# WHITEWAY'S CYDER

# WHITEWAY'S CYDER

## A COMPANY HISTORY

### E. V. M. WHITEWAY

**DAVID & CHARLES**
Newton Abbot London

British Library Cataloguing in Publication Data
Whiteway, E. V. M.
  Whiteway's cyder: a company history.
  1. England. Cider industries. Companies, history
  I. Title
  338.76632

  ISBN 0–7153–9819–9

Plates and Whiteway's ephemera from the collection of E. V. M. Whiteway

The right of E. V. M. Whiteway to be identified as author of this work
has been asserted by him in accordance with the Copyright, Designs and
Patents Act 1988

Printed in Great Britain
by Billings & Sons  Worcester
for David & Charles plc
Brunel House  Newton Abbot  Devon

*Dedicated to Henry Whiteway,*
*founder of the successful cyder company*
*at Whimple in Devon,*
*who made Whiteway's cyders well known*
*in Britain and around the world.*

# Contents

# A Devonshire Ceremony

On the eve of Twelfth Day it is the custom to go into the orchard with a large pitcher of cyder, and out of this each person takes a mug full of liquor. Standing under the best bearing apple tree, a toast is made:

Here's to thee, old apple tree,
Whence thou may'st bud, and whence thou may'st blow!
And whence thou may'st bear apples enow!
Hats full! caps full!
Bushel-bushel-sacks full,
And in my pockets full, too! Huzza!

# Introduction and Acknowledgements

I was born into a family which had made cyder in Devonshire for generations. As a small boy in the 1920s my early recollection of my grandfather, Henry Whiteway, was of a large and cheerful old man. My grandmother Edith Whiteway was, I felt, rather strict and, in the fashion of the time, usually wore a large hat. My grandfather's preferred drink was cyder, which he had prepared by the natural conditioning method in bottles, a process that was becoming obsolete.

My father was manager of the company's London office and factory, and we lived in Wimbledon where I attended school. Again, cyder was usually available and I enjoyed the non-alcoholic drink, Cydrax. There were frequent references in family conversations to some new product, or to the latest advertisements in newspapers or perhaps on the sides of the double-decker London buses. Occasionally visits were made to the factory at Vauxhall where the characteristic cyder smell was always present since the machines filled a multitude of bottles.

On visits to Whimple, Devon, I saw my uncle Ronald, who had recently returned from Nova Scotia to become general manager; his soft Canadian accent remained with him all his life. My other uncle, Herbert, had a son, Richard, about my own age, with whom I spent many holidays in the summer. We became familiar with the sight of the apple orchards, the farm carts laden with sacks of apples and, again, that pleasant cyder smell in the factory area.

The years spent at school, university and later in the Army overseas, passed, and both Richard and I joined the company.

9

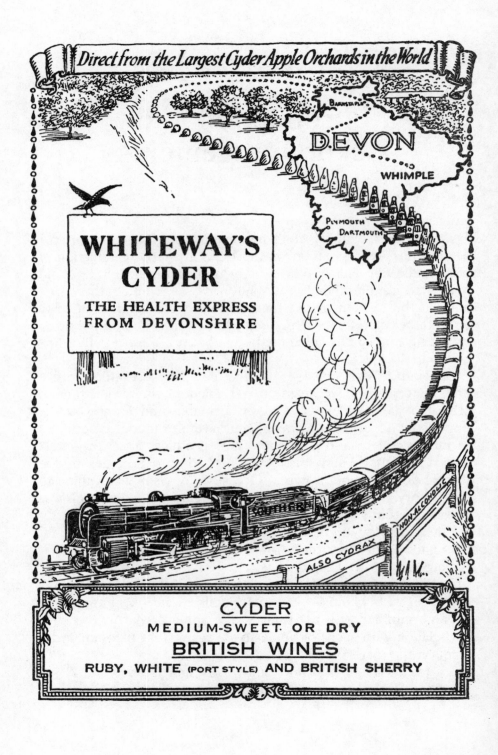

We had the desire to maintain and inspire the family traditions of the business.

For many years I have been assembling as much as possible of the early photographs, advertising material and other records which have contributed to the history of Whiteway's Devon cyders.

I would like to thank all those in the accounts, export and sales departments who have searched through old files and account books; the secretary of the National Association of Cider Makers who kindly provided information; and also Mary Fenner my former secretary for typing much of the manuscript.

Lastly, I must acknowledge the great help and assistance of Dennis Clapp, who joined this company in 1930, for checking many details during the preparation of the manuscript.

Eric Whiteway
1989

# THE·WINE·OF·THE·WEST·COVNTRY
# WHITEWAY'S
# FAMOUS·CYDERS

## WHIMPLE, DEVON. AND·22&23·ALBERT· EMBANKMENT, LONDON.

POMONA DEVONIENSIS

# 1

# In the Beginning

Cyder or cider has been known in England for at least 700 years. It is an alcoholic drink obtained by the fermentation of apple juice and usually has a strength of between 3 per cent and 6 per cent alcohol. Writing in 1898, C. W. R. Cook, MP, noted that the Ancient Phoenicians made *shekar* (meaning strong drink) believed to be cyder, and they may possibly have introduced it to northern Europe where apples grew indigenously. There are no references to cyder making during the Roman occupation of Britain, but after the Norman Conquest in 1066 the planting of orchards and making of cyder spread in many parts of England. The Greek *sikera*, Latin *sicera* (reference St Jerome, in the fourth century), meaning a strong

13

drink, gradually became sidir, sydar, seider etc, which forms are no longer used. There are some documentary references to cyder in the thirteenth and fourteenth centuries in Norfolk, Yorkshire and other counties. The most popular regions were Devonshire, Somerset and Herefordshire where cyder was made by local farmers with very rudimentary mills and presses. Cyder frequently formed part of farm labourers' wages until this practice was stopped by legislation in 1887.

We find that Sir Walter Raleigh, referring to his 1598 expedition, wrote to Sir John Gilbert ordering '. . . 50 toones of zider and 10,000 of Newfoundland fish'. This would have amounted to 10,000 gallons of cyder.

In the seventeenth century several books were published dealing with fruit growing and even describing new types of apple mills and presses. John Evelyn's *Sylva* (1664) is well known. J. Worlidge in *A Treatise of Cider* (1656) gave details of an iron drum mill set with short pegs not unlike some mills in use today. Richard Haynes (1674, London) wrote an article on making Cyder Royal which he stated '. . . may be made as strong, wholesome and pleasing as French wine'. He noted simple cyder was frequently sold for 30 shillings (£1.50) per hogshead or three halfpence per quart, whereas French wine sold for one shilling (5p) per quart. The name 'hogshead' for casks usually having a capacity of 50 to 70 gallons, came from a Scandinavian word meaning ox-hide.

Besides farmers, some country gentlemen became serious orchardists and made high quality cyders for their own households and perhaps also to impress their friends. Mr Batty Langley of Twickenham, London, produced a very large detailed and illustrated treatise on improving fruits, entitled *Pomona or The Fruit Garden Illustrated* (1729). The last chapter is by a gentleman named Hugh Stafford (1674–1734) who lived at Pynes near Exeter, Devon. Evidently a knowledgeable amateur cyder maker he related that, in about 1710, he noticed a wild crab-apple tree growing on the Exeter to Okehampton post road. He collected the fruit and later discovered that the cyder produced from them was quite outstanding and even comparable with Rhenish wine (hock). He gave it the name Royal Wilding and started to graft cuttings of it onto other trees. This Royal Wilding he thought superior to the Whitesour, a cyder apple renowned in the South Hams district near the Devon rivers Dart and Teign.

In 1763 Lord Bute, the Prime Minister, decided to impose a new flat-rate cyder duty of 4s (20p) per hogshead to be collected from the farmers. This immediately caused widespread protests and abuse from farmers in Devonshire and Herefordshire, since excise officers were given the right of entry to any farm. The simple cyder was then valued at 12s 6d (62p) per hogshead which meant the new tax was almost 30 per cent, whilst on the better cyder sold to merchants at 21s (£1.05) it was 20 per cent; this tax was payable within six weeks and was undoubtedly a severe setback, but it was not finally repealed until 1830.

In the middle of the nineteenth century the advent of railways enabled a cyder factory to transport casks and bottled cyder more easily to larger markets. In Devon, Henley & Sons had established a factory at the village of Abbotskerswell near Newton Abbot, and John Symons & Co had premises at The Plains, Totnes, not far away. H. P. Bulmer & Co was founded at Hereford in 1887, followed by William Gaymer and Son at Attleburgh, Norfolk, and Henry Whiteway & Co at Whimple near Exeter before the turn of the century. The National Association of English Cider Makers was formed in 1893 and The National Fruit and Cider Institute's research station, at Long Ashton near Bristol, in 1903. It was estimated that at this period the cyder growing counties had 116,000 acres of fruit, half of which were cyder varieties. In 1900 C. W. R. Cooke, MP, estimated (on rather unreliable statistics) that from 55 to 100 million gallons of cyder were produced. As late as 1920 some 5 million gallons came from factories and 16 million were still being made on farms, but in any case the figures showed a severe decrease since 1900. By the 1970s the orchard acreage had fallen to a little over 10,000, whereas by the 1980s, cyder sales, now dominated by several large factory producers, had risen again to record levels of over 60 million gallons per annum.

Orchards and Head Office :

WHIMPLE, DEVON.

London Office :

22 and 23, ALBERT EMBANKMENT, S.W.

Telephone 173 HOP.

*D*EAR SIR,

In presenting our Price List of the current year, we are pleased to be able to announce a most gratifying increase in business—notwithstanding the almost complete absence of summer weather—during 1909.

A more convincing proof of the fact that Whiteway's Cyders have increased in popularity as an all-the-year-round beverage could not be given. Our delicious Apple Wines, all of which we guarantee to be perfectly pure, have long been recognized as the safest and most satisfying summer drink ; and now, it would seem, Dame Nature herself has co-operated with us in our efforts to expose the fallacy that cyder is unsuitable as a winter beverage.

That this is a fallacy many of the most eminent medical authorities of the day have testified. For as all uric acid complaints become more prevalent and more acute during the winter, so a large number of our foremost practitioners have unhesitatingly affirmed that there is no better antidote for such troubles than Whiteway's Pure Dry Cyder.

It is undoubtedly due to the exceptional conditions of climate and soil in which our apples are grown, no less than the perfectly hygienic methods of manufacture, that our Whimple Cyders secure their unequalled popularity.

Never have we received more flattering encomiums than were accorded us in 1909. Furthermore, during that year our Royal patronage was continued on an increased scale.

Trusting that we may have an early opportunity of fulfilling your esteemed commands.

Yours faithfully,

Henry Whiteway

This book sets out to relate how Henry Whiteway founded the successful cyder industry at Whimple in Devon and made Whiteway's cyders well known throughout Britain and in many overseas markets.

'Cyder contains about the lowest percentage of alcohol of all popular fermented drinks. Unlike beer or any other malt liquor, it acts as an antidote to gout and to uric acid rheumatism. Vintage apples, as used for making Cyder, contain more tannin than the table fruit, and this imparts tonic properties to the liquor apart from its general astringent principle.'

*From* Meals Medicinal *by Dr W. T. Fernie and quoted in Whiteway's price list of 1910*

POMONA DEVONIENSIS

# 2

# The First Decade at Whimple to 1903

The family name of Whiteway can be traced back to the thirteenth century when a habitation of that name was established at Kingsteignton in south Devon. Over the centuries members of the family migrated to other parts of Devon. Henry Whiteway was born in 1853 at Luscombe Manor Farm, Harbertonford, near Totnes. His father, also Henry, born in 1810, had three daughters and one son. Their family tree, documented to the middle of the seventeenth century, shows almost all the men as being farmers and probably cyder makers in Devon. Young Henry was known as Harry to avoid confusion with his father, and farmed at

Luscombe, taking over from his father in 1878, the year that he married Edith Clift. Three sons were born at Harbertonford, Ronald 1885, Victor 1887 and Herbert 1891; Reginald was born in Whimple in 1896.

In 1891 the family moved to Churchill Farm near Whimple, a village in east Devon eight miles from Exeter. Henry's wife Edith was the only daughter of Edward Clift who had owned farms and property in Whimple throughout the middle of the nineteenth century. After they had settled at Churchill, Edward Clift, then aged 84, came to live with his daughter and family. Edith Whiteway was born at Whimple and knew it well from childhood times and so probably was the one who persuaded Henry to move to the village she loved. Henry Whiteway, then aged 38, was well trained by his father in the traditional skills of selecting cyder apples and making cyders at the farm. The established Devonshire cyder firms such as Henley & Sons of Newton Abbot and J. Symons & Co of Totnes, were well known locally, and would have been familiar to him.

In the 1880s farming was in a somewhat depressed state and even cyder sales were in decline. Nevertheless Henry Whiteway had a vision of creating a modern and efficient cyder industry together with the scientific orchard management necessary to improve the supply and quality of the cyder fruit.

Edward Clift died at Whimple in 1894 and this enabled his orchards and other land, some of which he had owned since the 1850s, to be transferred to the new cyder business. Whimple is recorded in the Devonshire Domesday book (1085) and is situated along the Roman road, now the A30 trunk road to London. The soil is basically clay with some sandstone, which was found to be suitable for growing orchard fruit as well as for grazing, on gentle undulating pastures.

A former tanyard, which was a brick building on three floors, was acquired as well as a nearby thatched barn beside a stream; known as The Cranny, these buildings became the press house and cyder cellars before the end of the century. The tanyard once had a water-wheel but Henry Whiteway preferred to use a steam engine to power the mill, press and other plant. Meanwhile an acre of land, part of the Slewton estate, and conveniently situated beside Whimple Station on the London & South Western Railway main line (opened in 1862) was earmarked for the new factory. In 1899 the Whiteway family moved to a house called The Cypresses adjoining the tanyard building.

## THE APPLE SUPPLY

A great many of the mixed farms of east Devon already had mature apple orchards including a mixture of cyder varieties. Henry Whiteway had inherited some orchards from his father-in-law but it was essential to buy additional supplies each autumn from an area of ten miles or more from the factory. By the 1890s a convenient railway goods service covered the area and the farmers normally took their bagged apples by horse and wagon to the nearest station, Honiton or Broadclyst or Ottery as convenient, for delivery to Whimple. There were often complaints about the high goods charges, but as there were no alternative means of transport farmers had to use the railway. Cyder apple varieties grown in Devon included Tom Putt; Woodbine; Crimson King; Kingston Black; Yarlington Mill; Sweet Alford; Sweet Coppin; Sweet Cluster; Star o' Devon and Fair Maid of Devon. One of the characteristics of cyder apples is a higher tannin content and lower acidity than those grown for eating or cooking. Over a period Henry Whiteway built up a list of farmers on whose crop he could rely for quality each season, there being forty-seven suppliers in 1897. The cyder pressing season commenced in early October and continued through until December or occasionally January. The price paid for cyder fruit ranged from £1 per ton to more than £3 per ton delivered to Whimple. In the early years the quantities pressed varied from less than 500 tons to more than 1,000 tons in the season.

## SELLING THE PRODUCT

Before an alcoholic product could be sold, an excise licence was required from the local justices. A firm of solicitors, Ford, Harris and Ford of Exeter was engaged to facilitate this formality.

Henry Whiteway certainly envisaged his Devonshire cyders

being sold throughout the United Kingdom and overseas. He decided to place a number of small advertisements in local and national daily newspapers inviting readers to write for samples and prices. Private customers and trade customers, of course, were desired equally by the new cyder business. An enquiry from Exeter was quoted one shilling (5p) per gallon on rail in 1895 and another in Staffordshire 1s 4d (7p) on rail. The Torquay brewery was quoted similar prices but W. Trump, a grocer in Sidmouth, Devon, only 8d (3p).

Another idea was to hire a stand for promoting Whiteway's Cyders at agricultural shows such as the Bath & West or the Devon County. The caterers to the show might also be persuaded to accept a quotation for sole supplies of cyder.

Then there were agents, who were usually freelance salesmen working on a commission basis, probably for more than one firm, but not in a competitive type of product. Some agents were appointed in various cities – Manchester, Plymouth or London – in order to introduce Whiteway's cyders to trade customers. One of these was A.C. Collier, who lived at Reigate, Surrey.

In 1897 Henry Whiteway entered into a partnership with Mr Alban E. Bellairs of Gerrards Cross, Bucks, when the firm became known as Henry Whiteway & Company.

Alban Bellairs was clearly a man of many interests with useful connections in London and elsewhere; he soon became a most energetic salesman of the Whimple cyders. At that period cyder in general was not always very drinkable and most gentlemen preferred wine; others favoured beer or spirits. Bellairs had the entrée to a wide circle of professional people – medical, legal, sporting – in golf clubs, sailing clubs and in commerce. Rupert D'Oyly Carte of the Savoy operas showed much interest in Whiteway's cyders. Well known schools, such as Eton and Harrow, were included for orders.

One successful way was to enlarge on Henry Whiteway's early method and advertise in a variety of newspapers and journals (*The Daily Telegraph, The Standard, Bazaar & Mart, Homoeopathic World* etc) inviting readers to send for samples. A considerable amount of correspondence and numerous orders from all parts of Britain ensued. These orders were generally from private individuals and goods were despatched by rail in returnable casks or, if bottled cyder, in wooden cases, the empties being credited on return to Whimple Station, LSWR.

Alban Bellairs also wrote numerous personal letters to eminent friends and acquaintances who received sample cases of assorted bottled cyders for their opinion. Glowing testimonials began to arrive at the company's office comparing Whiteway's bottled brands with champagne, but more economical.

Trade shows were regularly supported with stands at the brewers' exhibitions and at food exhibitions, as well as various agricultural shows. The price list of 1900 is given below.

*Dry sparkling*

**Price per dozen bottles**

| | |
|---|---|
| Whimple Pomona | 15s (75p) Old, medium dry. |
| Woodbine blend | 12s (60p) Very delicate and dry. Recommended by medical profession. |
| Fair Maid of Devon | 10s (50p) Slightly dry; from red apples. |
| Whimple Specialité | 8s 6d (42p) Extra dry. |

*Sweet Sparkling*

| | |
|---|---|
| Sweet Alford | 12s (60p) Fine fruity, rich and full. |
| Whimple Specialité | 7s 6d (37p) Medium sweet. |

*Still*

| | |
|---|---|
| Dartmoor | 20s (£1) Dry, 7 years old. |
| Exe Valley | 15s (75p) Full 4 years old. |
| Apple Sauterne | 8s (40p) Smooth full bodied. |

*Perry*

| | |
|---|---|
| Oldfield | 12s (60p) Medium; from pear juice. |

All of these drinks were guaranteed to be pure juice of Devon apples without addition of any chemicals.

Alban Bellairs was able to enlist the help of his nephews, R.H. Bellairs in Oxford and Mowbray Bellairs, both of whom sent orders for cyder to Whimple.

## EARLY EXPORT TRADE

In 1898 Henry Whiteway obtained *The Mercantile Year Book*, a directory for exporters at 7s 6d (37p). In due course this led to correspondence with several firms willing to try the Whimple cyder brands. In September 1898 in Guernsey, J.P. Pells, an agent for J.A. Devenish and Company, brewers, placed an order. In October, Phipson & Company of Bombay, India reported they could sell Whiteway's cyders at 8 rupees per dozen quarts and 5 rupees 4 annas for pints. By November, B. Smyth & Company Limited of New China Bazaar Street, Calcutta, were showing interest, and later Edward Levy & Company of Billiter Street, London EC had sent samples to Australia. On 8 December 1898 The Borneo Company Limited, Fenchurch Street, London, wrote that they were to explore the situation for cyder in Singapore, and on 13 December Mr A. Stanley Hill c/o Standard Bank, Cape Town, South Africa, was considered as agent for cyder. In the same month Dyer and Dyer, Shipping Agents, ordered ten 18 gallon casks of 1895 vintage cyder, at 1s 6d per gallon, for loading at Southampton to East London, South Africa by the Union Steamship Company.

## ENLARGING THE FACTORY

The successful selling initiatives were soon followed by the need for more storage capacity and for improved facilities for bottling and packing of orders. Farm cyder makers generally used 60 gallon oak hogsheads or 120 gallon oak pipes, both for fermenting the apple juice and later racking it off into clean vessels for maturing and storage. Ideally these were stacked in rows, perhaps two or more high, in a barn or cellar. Sales had now reached 100,000 gallons per annum requiring a stock of about 2,000 hogsheads. These were easily purchased from wine shippers in England who accumulated empties from the port and sherry imports.

In 1898 it was decided to build new cyder cellars and a press house with an office building. Charles Cole, an Exeter architect, was engaged for this, and a brick and tiled building, partly on three floors, was erected on the road frontage of the one acre field adjoining Whimple Station. The original estimate was for £260. This building, still part of the factory complex, continued in use for ninety years. The following year a new apple press, together with apple handling elevators, was installed at a cost of £575. This work was carried out by H. Beare and Sons of Newton Abbot, a firm of agricultural engineers with experience in supplying cyder-making plant throughout Devon. In the absence of electrical power a steam engine was used to drive the shafting belts and pulleys which operated the various apple elevators, mills and conveyors.

During the making season, apples were conveyed to the upper floor by a moving bucket elevator and then delivered onto a hopper feeding the mill which rotated at 2,000 rpm and reduced them to a pulp. The next stage was to apply a high pressure to express the juice whilst retaining the skins and solid matter.

The new press had a fixed rectangular base approximately 5ft square, made of heavy timber. A strong steel frame supported the overhead moving platen, which was forced downwards by a screw-driven toggle arm device.

The milled apple pulp was spread with rakes over a coarse woollen cloth, folded over and laid within a light wooden lattice frame. This was repeated ten or twelve times to build up the 'cheese' to a height of about 5ft. The power pulley was then set in motion to bring the top platen down heavily, causing the juice to flow out through the cloths into the receiving vessel. A ton of apples could yield as much as 170 gallons of juice.

Henry Whiteway always insisted on the strictest cleanliness of cyder-making plant, vats and hogsheads. Steam-heated water, often with sulphur dioxide, was the method used. The presence of unwanted bacteria or metallic residues could spoil the finest cyders and the hygiene system was regarded as essential. Fermentation was allowed to take place quite naturally from the yeasts always present on the skins of the apples and, provided the temperature was controlled, would continue for three or four weeks until most of the sugar had been converted into alcohol. The sugar content of the juice was checked by hydrometer. A reading of 1.040 was low, whereas 1.070 was high and produced a stronger cyder.

In the nineteenth and early twentieth centuries the usual method of bottling sparkling cyder was the natural conditioning process. A carefully blended cyder which contained a certain reserve of sugar and yeast was bottled in early spring of the year and the cork firmly secured by a wire. It should be explained that it was necessary to use champagne bottles (75cl) which had thick glass capable of withstanding a pressure of over 100lb/sq inch. When the warmer weather arrived, a secondary fermentation had taken place in the bottles giving the cyder that delightful 'champagne-like' effervescence. Such naturally conditioned cyder, however, tended to throw a sediment or exhibit a slight haze which would not be found acceptable in the 1990s.

At the new cyder cellars, Whiteway's bottled, corked, labelled and applied smart tinfoil decoration to thousands of champagne bottles. A new bottle-washing machine was obtained to cleanse the steady flow of returned empties arriving every week by rail. This machine, a rotary soaker and rinser type, was supplied by L. Lumley and Company, America Square, Minories, London in December 1897 and cost £15 10s 0d (£15.50). The dirty bottles were soaked in hot water with soda and a rotary brush cleaned the inside, finally a clean water jet rinsed inside and out. There were a number of bottlers in the trade who bought hogsheads of special bottling cyder in January or February each year and filled their own bottles for local sale, some being under their own label.

Another firm of engineers, Barnett and Foster, Eagle Wharf, London N, supplied carbonating machines with silver-plated internal fittings, also corking machines and other bottlers' sundries. The alternative method of rendering cyder sparkling required the use of carbon dioxide gas supplied in cylinders and a suitable injection device for introducing it into the cyder. This was quicker and more reliable than the old method and could be used all year round.

# EMPLOYEES

The village of Whimple, with a population of less than 1,000, was able to provide the modest staff of about twelve men and a few women for the various simple processes and bottling operations.

Village facilities at the end of the nineteenth century were negligible. Water could be obtained only from shallow wells or from a river, there was no main drainage system, and mains electricity was still a generation into the future. The Post Office provided the usual mail and telegraph facility, a village policeman lived in the vicinity and patrolled on his bicycle. The rector of the ancient church conducted religious observances and gave some social service to the community, supported by the minister of a chapel. The national school provided elementary education. The roads were still surfaced with rolled stone cracked by hand, dusty in summer and muddy in winter. In the unlikely event of a motor car appearing in Whimple it would have been viewed with awe and wonder by the villagers.

It was probably the London & South Western Railway which, after the 1860s, brought the possibility of rapid travel and a form of technology to the people of east Devon. The gramophone and cinematograph, however, were still a few years away.

The names of employees included in early photographs are recorded. Mr Potter became foreman, and then there were Messrs J. Davey, Greenaway, Hayman, Horrell, Bill Hutchings, Jack Hutchings, Pollard, Snooks, Symes, Ellis Clements and Mrs Symes.

Wages paid to those on cyder making were related to the current agricultural rates in the area. The weekly wage for adult men was 13s 10d to 15s (69p to 75p) for about fifty-two hours. Women's rates were usually about half those amounts. In 1901 a branch was opened in London at 22 and 23 Albert Embankment, Vauxhall. Mr Potter and his family moved to London where he was foreman for more than thirty years.

In the same year, Mr A. Langman joined the Whimple office as accountant, assisted by Messrs Godfrey and C. Pope. Langman later became chief accountant; he retired in 1946.

At the end of November 1900 sales had reached £6,744, with assets of £9,580; net profit on trading was £2,634. The partners, Henry Whiteway and A.E. Bellairs, each received share of profit at £1,238.

27

## "A NICE GLASS OF WINE JACK?"

"Rather! But what's happened, mother. Has dad won the pool at last?"

"No, worse luck! But we've found a real honest-to-goodness full-strength British Wine at a reasonable price—I mean you can't say that one and ninepence per bottle is exactly robbery, can you?"

"Really! But how can they do it, and who does it anyway?"

"Well! It's made by Whiteways and that's a name we know and respect. They import the Grape Juice direct from the Vineyards, make the Wine in Sunny Devon, and so do not pay Duty as on foreign Wines."

"Well! Whiteway's name on the bottle is good enough for me, and there is nothing like a glass of Wine for bucking a fellow up."

Whiteway's Wines, approved by the Royal Institute of Public Health and Hygiene, are recommended by many doctors as a restorative.

# WHITEWAY's

**PORT STYLE WINES** (RUBY & WHITE)
**AND BRITISH SHERRY**

CVS—23

POMONA DEVONIENSIS

# 3

# A Day in the Life of a Cyder Maker

At the end of the nineteenth century most Devon farmers were still making their cyder on the farm with the old mills and hand presses of their forefathers.

At Whimple, however, things had changed. Mr Potter, Whiteway's foreman and a large man in his prime, had worked for the new firm for several years and had seen the new building completed in 1899 and the new plant installed. The pressing season began in late September or October as signs of autumn were appearing and often continued until Christmas.

While he lived in the village Mr Potter walked to work in good time to start by 7am, by which hour the other men and a few girls had walked or cycled to the factory for work. When the steam boiler for the engine was required, Jack Hutchings had to arrive earlier to stoke the fire and get up steam ready to drive the new apple elevators, mill and the mechanical press. Across the road, at the railway goods yard, some bags of apples waited in trucks, and Mr Potter would remind Ellis Clements, who handled the horse and cart, to go and fetch a load down to the factory. Other men (Symes, Horrell and Whiscombe) would be getting ready the stack of cloths, racks and the flat trucks for the press. Jack Hutchings, the 'engineer', checked the belt drives on the various pulleys, gave the greasers a turn or two and told Mr Potter that everything was in order to start.

Belts were shifted over from the loose to the fast pulleys, screeching a little as they conveyed the load of apples in the elevator up to the third floor. There they dropped into the rapidly rotating mill which reduced them to a soft pulp (pomace) on the way to an open vat on the floor below. Meanwhile, three men on the ground floor spread a heavy, coarse, blanket-like cloth over the flat truck beside the press ready to receive the apple pomace from above. A layer was quickly spread with wooden rakes and the cloth folded over, a rack placed on top and the whole process repeated ten or twelve times. The 'cheese', as it was called, dripping with apple juice, was then pushed under the great press. One of the men moved the drive belt that started the screw device turning. Down came the top platen forcing out streams of juice, which were collected in a tank below the floor.

As the day wore on more local farmers brought their cyder apples in horse-drawn wagons; the sacks had to be checked by Mr Potter and then unloaded and weighed. Henry Whiteway, together with his clerks, Godfrey and Pope, would have arrived at the office to deal with the day's post and to arrange despatch of the orders by rail.

In those days the men went to work dressed in heavy woollen breeches or trousers, often with leather leggings and strong boots with iron studs, woollen shirts and usually a waistcoat. Most men wore a cap and Mr Potter's resembled that of a naval petty officer. The girls were dressed in ankle-length dresses, white aprons and hats – even when engaged in bottling work.

A stop for breakfast at about 9am was welcome when the men usually had a pint of cyder with their food. A short 'toot' on the steam engine whistle called for a return to work.

Mr Potter had to make sure that the empty hogsheads and pipes (120 gallons) had been thoroughly cleaned out and were ready for the new juice, together with the hose pipe and semi-rotary hand pumps to fill them. These oak casks were stored both inside and outside in the orchard in long rows, two high. In mild weather fermentation soon began quite naturally, in frosty weather it was slower.

The other men and girls operated the machine for soaking and washing the bottles, which were then filled with cyder. A hand-operated machine forced in the corks, which had to be secured with wires then decorated with tinfoil, and the bottles labelled ready for despatch. From time to time Henry Whiteway went out to inspect the progress of cyder pressing and bottling in the factory. Another break was taken in the middle of the day.

In the early years water was always a problem because the steam boiler required a regular supply. An iron pipe had been laid through the orchard to the stream at the other end and when required one of the men had to pump the water. Clean water for such purposes as bottle washing was pumped from a well, but the amount which could be extracted was limited.

As the afternoon light faded, Mr Potter would have the hurricane lamps lighted and hung up in various places. These were usually supplemented by naphtha flares which gave quite a good but smoky light. A tea-time break came in the afternoon when, again, the men preferred to drink rough cyder.

Depending on the supply of cyder apples which had arrived, pressing would continue until 5pm or 6pm. In 1900 the factory pressed over 1,000 tons in this manner during the season.

Mr Potter would then see that the mill, press, cloths and racks had been carefully scrubbed down and left ready for the following day's work, and the boiler fire shut down. Then he would lock up and go home.

The process of cyder making eighty years later has changed almost beyond comparison. Heavy lorries now arrive with fifteen or twenty tonnes of apples in bulk, usually loose rather than in bags. The apples are tipped into hoppers and conveyed along water canals to the conveyors, where stainless steel mills driven, of course, by electric motors are ready to crush them. The pomace is then pumped to the great automatic hydraulic stainless steel presses. The tiled walls of the press house shine, the fluorescent lighting casts a soft illumination, the non-slip floors are relatively free of pomace, and a small number of operators can control the operations by pressing buttons. The juice is checked by laboratory technicians, whilst the fermentations take place in large metal vats. Quality is assured by special yeasts grown and cultured to the specification of the particular cyders to be marketed.

Mr Potter would be very surprised.

POMONA DEVONIENSIS

# 4

# The New Company 1904–18

The advent of the twentieth century saw the business established and growing steadily. In 1899 Henry Whiteway had moved to a house then known as The Cypresses situated on the western boundary of Whimple and close to the tanyard and the new factory buildings. In 1901 premises had been acquired at 22 to 23 Albert Embankment, Vauxhall, London SW. This was to provide a sales office for expansion of the business in the metropolis and in due course was to become a branch store and bottling depot for despatch of cyder in the London area and to other parts of the United Kingdom, served by the railways radiating from London. Small storage depots were also rented in Leeds and Glasgow, for a better service in the north. The freight services by rail from

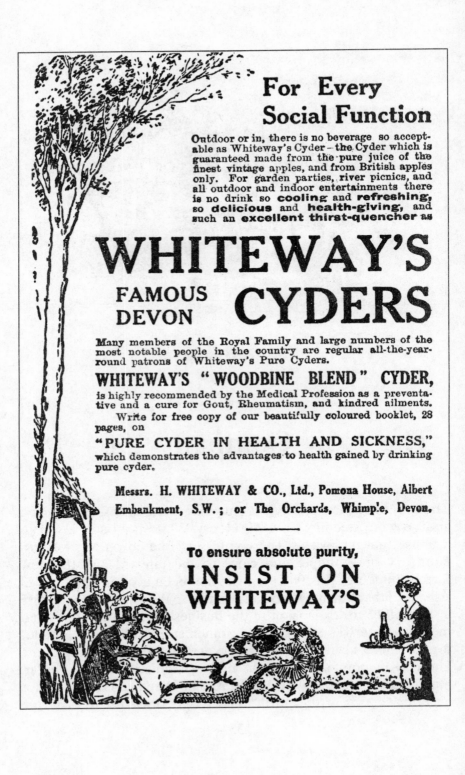

Whimple Station to London were very efficient. Truckloads of cyder in hogsheads loaded by the afternoon were delivered to Nine Elms goods depot, Vauxhall and thence by horse-drawn vans early the next morning to the company's store at nearby Albert Embankment.

In 1903 it was felt that the time had come to form a private company for the further expansion of the business. Alban Bellairs, Henry Whiteway's partner since 1897, who had been most successful in promoting the sales and introducing many valuable new accounts, decided to withdraw rather than join the new company.

Henry Whiteway & Co Ltd was incorporated on 4 January 1904. The initial capital was £25,000 with shares of £1. The original subscribers were:

Henry Whiteway, The Cypresses, Whimple, Devon
Edith Whiteway, wife of Henry Whiteway
Ronald Harry Clift Whiteway, clerk to Henry Whiteway & Co
Arthur Langman, Whimple, Devon clerk and accountant
   to Henry Whiteway & Co
William John Harris, Exeter, accountant
Frank Kennedy Sharland, Exeter, accountant

The first directors were required to have £100 in shares. Henry Whiteway became chairman and managing director, and Edith and Ronald Whiteway, directors. The solicitors for the company were Ford, Harris and Ford of Exeter, which firm, later known as Ford, Simey and Ford, remains the company's legal advisor today. Auditors were Denman and Allen of Yeovil, later Chalmers Wade, who continued in office for seventy years. The bank at that time was the Devon and Cornwall Banking Co Ltd, Exeter, later to be absorbed by Lloyds Bank Ltd.

The company was authorised to carry on business in any part of the world as apple and pear merchants, cyder, perry and vinegar manufacturers, wine and spirit merchants, wholesale and retail, manufacturers of pickles and jams, coopers and bottlers, bottle makers, manufacturers and dealers in aerated and mineral waters and other drinks.

In 1905 a financial stake was acquired in the Annapolis Valley Cyder Co Ltd of Bridgetown, Nova Scotia, Canada. Ronald Whiteway, aged 20, went to live in Nova Scotia to assist that company and in later years became the manager. In 1913 he married Alice de Witt of New York. He was able to learn much of American advertising and business methods, but he also returned to England every year to keep in touch with the activities at Whimple. He eventually returned for good to the Whiteway's head office in 1921 when the company's interests in Annapolis Valley Cyder Co were sold.

Meanwhile Henry Whiteway bought a house at Kennington Oval, near Vauxhall, so that he could spend more time at the increasingly busy London office. This involved much commuting by train between Vauxhall station and Whimple, both of which were on the London main line of L&SW Railway.

In the early 1900s people travelled in London either by the London County Council electric trams, or by London General petrol buses, horse cabs or by one of the few motor taxis. Goods were almost invariably conveyed by horse-drawn transport or, for longer distances, by railway goods services.

In 1905 Henry Whiteway moved again, this time to Fordton House which overlooked the cyder factory land.

# SALES 1904

The selling plan, or as it would be termed today, the marketing scheme, was designed to convince readers that Whiteway's Devon cyders were absolutely pure, free from additives and therefore healthy and pleasurable to drink. The quality was guaranteed, cyder was a beverage for every occasion, a rival to and far more economical than foreign wines, in fact the wine of England.

For advertising, the medium used was the national press, local press, and periodicals of all kinds. Cyder always sold far better in the summer, the warmer the weather the greater the demand, so advertisements appeared from May onwards. The local papers included *The Express and Echo* (Exeter), *Devon and Exeter Gazette*, and *The Western Morning News*, using the slogan '. . . the native wine of England'. National dailies such as

*The Guardian* and *The Daily Telegraph* '. . . for social occasions, garden parties etc', '. . . ideal summer drink, beer and spirits too heavy – aerated waters too gassy – foreign wines too costly'. *The Tatler* informed readers that Whiteway's Cyder could be obtained from leading wine merchants, stores, licensed grocers from 4 shillings (20p) per dozen champagne pints. Advertisements, size 7 x 5in, appeared in *The Bystander, Graphic, The Guardian, Illustrated London News, The Sketch, The Sphere* and *The Daily Telegraph*. Smaller classified announcements were placed in *The Daily Chronicle, Daily Express, Daily Graphic, Daily Mail, Daily Mirror, The Mercury Post, Daily News, The Evening Standard, The Times* and, again, *The Daily Telegraph*.

Woodbine Blend was a dry cyder which was generally considered to be beneficial to sufferers from gout and rheumatic complaints. Numerous letters supporting this view were received from the medical profession. *The Lancet* wrote '. . . the cyders which are of distinct merit and which may be trusted for their soundness of condition are those produced in the orchards at Whimple in Devon'. From S. Gilbert MD, Reigate '. . . all your brands are good, I prefer the Woodbine for the rheumatic and gouty'. D. Dyce-Brown MD, British Medical Association, Portman Square, London '. . . there is now no excuse for not prescribing cyder where it can be got so pure and agreeable and we strongly recommend our colleagues to try it as a beverage instead of beer or wine and to test its value as an article of diet in gouty patients. The proprietors are Henry Whiteway & Co, Whimple, Devon'.

The temperance movement was active during this period. Promoted by the Salvation Army and other religious bodies in order to combat excessive drinking habits among some sections of the public, Henry Whiteway decided to introduce a new non-alcoholic apple drink which was named Cydrax. The first label design was registered on 4 July 1902. Cydrax was supplied as a carbonated drink in a bottle. It was described as a pure non-alcoholic beverage made chiefly from apples and containing no chemicals whatsoever. It was destined to become a well known brand throughout Britain and many overseas countries during the next eighty years.

Cydrax was heavily promoted but principally directed at the temperance movement and churches. Described as cyder without alcohol, periodicals included the *Christian World, Methodist Times, Methodist Recorder, Church Family Newspaper, The Church Commonwealth, Baptist Times, The Presbyterian, The Friend, The Church Herald, Everyman, Life of Faith, The Record, The Church Evangelist, Joyful News, The Christian Globe, Church Times, Temperance Chronicles* and others. Even in the *Islamic Review* it was stated '. . . all Muslims may drink Cydrax'.

In 1912 a speciality apple liqueur was added to the range of cyders under the name Pomvita. The contemporary write-up stated '. . . Pomvita could be taken hot or cold or mixed with effervescing waters'. Testimonials included that of A. Shaw of Whalley Range, '. . . The Pomvita did more than please me, it delighted me, and I, like Oliver Twist wanted more'. Another, from A. Wolf-Murray, Harrogate, '. . . I like your Pomvita better than Port which I have drunk for more than 50 years'. This product did not sell as well as expected, however, and was later withdrawn.

In 1903 a contract was signed with Spiers and Pond Ltd of London, a well known firm of wine merchants and refreshment contractors in the United Kingdom. This provided for sole supplies of Whiteway's cyders in bottle or draught to all their permanent establishments including the London & South Western Railway for five years. The contract was renewed over many years and later Cydrax supplies were included.

Advertising continued in all kinds of periodicals and by 1914 *The Car Illustrated, The Field, Ladies' Field, London Opinion, Punch* and *Truth* were used for advertising cyder. An advertisement even appeared in Welsh in *The Celt* as below:

Y DDIOD, OREU AR HIN BOETH
SEIDYR ENWOG DEVON WHITEWAY
MYNNWCH SEIDYR WHITEWAY

The Great War started on 4 August 1914 and on the 16 August Whiteway's had taken an advertisement in *The Army Service Gazette*. In December another followed in *The Daily Telegraph*:

38

'be patriotic this Christmas, banish all German hocks and lager beers – drink Whiteway's Devonshire Cyders'.

The export trade was not forgotten and supplies continued to be imported by agents in India, South America, Africa, and elsewhere. It was even claimed that cyder was the only beverage suitable for *mal-de-mer* (sea sickness). Eminent customers mentioned were Lady Wingate of the Palace, Khartoum, and George Sanders Esq, the British Embassy, Berlin. For many years agents in India were Phipson and Co, Bombay; Cutler Palmer & Co, Lahore; and Murray & Co, Karachi.

# EMPLOYEES

In 1905, Henry Whiteway's second son, Victor (born 1887) started his career with the firm, and quite soon went to Nova Scotia to assist his elder brother Ronald at the Annapolis Valley Cyder Company.

By 1909 the London office was still not large and amounted to twelve employees in the depot and three on the clerical side. Total weekly wages were about £19. Frank Thorn Hatley joined the office in 1911 as office 'boy'. Little could he have known then that his career was to continue for more than fifty years until he retired as a director and London manager in 1965. This long period of service was only interrupted by army service between 1914 and 1918. Victor Whiteway returned from Nova Scotia in 1913 and took charge of the London premises at Vauxhall.

The staff at the Whimple factory now numbered about thirty men and women, rising to forty by 1913. The apple orchards were gradually increasing in acreage as more land was acquired and trees planted. These and other farming activities were entrusted to Ellis Clements as farm bailiff, who remained with the company until the post-war years.

Herbert Whiteway, Henry Whiteway's third son, commenced work at Whimple in 1909 and began specialising in the cyder making, bottling and transport side of the business. He later became production director and remained with the company until his death in 1959.

The youngest son, Reginald, joined the firm at Whimple in

# A Few Facts about Whiteway's Cyders.

**They do not cause headiness** as do beer or spirits even when diluted with mineral waters.

**They are a certain antidote,** if not a cure, for gout, rheumatism, gravel, &c., and are recommended as such by the highest medical authorities.

**They are healthiest for business men**—and for all who, leading sedentary lives, are apt to suffer from sluggish liver—because of the phosphorous and tonic acids the apples contain.

**They are guaranteed pure and free** from chemicals.

**They are moderate in prices.** Even our special varieties, so sparkling, light, and clean to the palate, are cheaper than foreign wines of repute, which they at least equal in quality; while our popular brands are no dearer than the best beers or stout.

1913, but very soon the war came and he volunteered for the Devonshire Regiment.

There were many employees at Whimple whose long service should be recorded – Herbert White who eventually became works manager and retired in 1946. Wilfred Maddocks, a lad who became a cooper, worked for the firm for over fifty years and retired in 1960. Joe Woodley, who became cellar foreman and cyder expert, exceeded fifty years, and his brother Sid served for not much less. Bill Wheaton, who must have filled hundreds of thousands of casks of cyder, stayed for forty years. One could go on with many more names of those Devon men and women who worked long hours, 55 or 60 hours per week, and whose holidays were at that time little more than the Christmas, Easter and statutory bank holidays.

The agricultural wages in 1914 were approximately 16s 9d (84p) per week rising in 1918 to £1 10s 6d (152p).

## THE GREAT WAR 1914–18

In August 1914 many people thought the war would be over in a few months, but by 1915 men were leaving to enlist in the army or navy. Victor Whiteway joined the East Surrey Regiment, Herbert, The Honourable Artillery Company and Reginald the Devonshire Regiment. F.W. Dyer who was not fit for military service went to the London office for the duration. Later he became the sales office manager at Whimple until he died suddenly at the age of 53.

The Government introduced a 'war tax' on cyder in 1915 at a flat rate of one shilling (5p) per dozen quarts or 5d (2p) per gallon draught. This tax was not removed until 1923 and cyder thereafter remained tax free for nearly forty years when purchase tax at 15 per cent was applied in May 1962. As the war went into the third and fourth year, supplies of beer and spirits were severely curtailed partly due to the fact that grains needed for their production were diverted for essential food requirements and also perhaps because of the government's concern at widespread drunkenness. Restrictions on the opening hours of public houses and bars were introduced for that reason. Imported wines were also in short supply because of priority on shipping space for war purposes and the unavailability of German and East European supplies. The English cyder makers, however, used indigenous apples and had no need to use imported materials, which enabled Whiteway's to continue, subject to increasing manpower shortage and war time restrictions on fuel and many other commodities.

Business was still divided between numerous direct private customers and increasing numbers of wholesale and retail accounts and local agents in most towns. There were also considerable numbers of retailers who preferred to buy hogsheads of draught cyder which they bottled locally.

In 1917 government restrictions prohibited the sending of circulars to private customers. Consequently 2,250 letters had to be despatched requesting that orders should be sent in future to Whiteway's Whimple or London offices. In 1918 and 1919 sales increased to record levels in spite of all the difficulties. The 1918 apple crop was almost a complete failure and the price was fixed by the government at £20 per ton, or ten times the usual figure for cyder apples. The crop the following year was excellent and the price returned to £4 per ton. The average annual purchases had amounted to 1,350 tons at prices varying from £1 in 1912 to £2 15s 0d (£2.75) per ton in 1917. But the 60 per cent excess profits tax imposed during the war largely offset these increases and by the end of the war business was thriving.

| Year | Sales | Profit before Tax |
|------|-------|-------------------|
| 1904 | £16,840 | £6,757 |
| 1911 | £35,880 | £16,220 |
| 1919 | £60,544 | £28,755 |

POMONA DEVONIENSIS

# 5

# The Inter-war Years

Henry Whiteway suffered a great loss in 1918 when news arrived that his son Captain Victor Whiteway, MC had died of wounds in France.

It was therefore decided that Reginald, the youngest son, now demobilised from the army, should take charge of the company's London premises at Vauxhall. Reginald Whiteway had married Kathleen Morgan of Whimple in 1917, and, together with their infant son, Eric, the family went to live in Wimbledon, early in 1920. The frequent electric train service took about a quarter of an hour to cover the distance from Wimbledon to Vauxhall (Southern Railway), and Reginald Whiteway was usually at the office by 7.30am.

Frank Hatley, also demobilised, returned to the London office and together with three in the office and about twenty-three in the factory, they set about the post-war reconstruction. In 1921 Henry Whiteway's financial interests in the Canadian Cyder Company in Nova Scotia were sold and Ronald Whiteway returned to the Whimple head office.

The cyder trade was very seasonal and sales increased greatly during a hot summer, followed by much reduced activity after Christmas until Easter. In order to occupy the salesmen during the winter period a new venture was tried. This was an alcoholic ginger wine purchased from another manufacturer in bulk and bottled by Whiteway's under their own label. The price was 2s 3d (11p) per bottle.

Henry Whiteway had reached seventy years of age in 1923 and considered the time had come to appoint his son Ronald as general manager, although he remained a director of the company.

In March 1920, members of the cyder making industry decided to form the National Association of Cyder Makers. E. F. Bulmer was elected chairman, Mr W. C. Henley, vice chairman, E. Bond, honorary secretary and treasurer. The executive committee elected included Messrs W. C. Gaymer, E. Bond (William Evans & Co Ltd), W. D. McCreath (Carr & Quick Limited), Symons and Henry Whiteway. This association, after nearly seventy years, still meets regularly and is more active than ever in considering new legislation and all matters affecting the cyder industry.

Henry Whiteway became chairman for the period 1924-25. In the late 1920s he and his wife Edith retired to live at Exmouth, a seaside resort near Exeter.

The London depot at 37 Albert Embankment, Vauxhall, now began to assume a major role in the expansion of the cyder business both in the metropolis and beyond. Reginald Whiteway introduced a dynamic management which ensured that customers' orders were delivered the next day or, in some cases, the same day as received. Frank Hatley, Reginald Whiteway and a new West End of London sales representative, W. E. Calow, called on prospective customers. The wartime cyder duty was removed in May 1923, enabling lower prices to be restored.

The new general manager, Ronald Whiteway, travelled to London every week to discuss sales promotion schemes with his brother Reginald, and with the advertising and other firms engaged for printing the various leaflets and letters to agents. Sales were now directed to the normal trade channels through wholesalers, retailers and others rather than to private customers as in the early years.

Export sales to India, Africa, Egypt, Persia, Australia, Japan, China, Mesopotamia and Spanish speaking countries were also managed from the London depot. Export orders almost always required modifications to the printing or supplementary labels for bottles as well as heavy duty cases to withstand rough handling on docksides.

Herbert L. Whiteway also returned from war service and in 1919 married Dorothy Morgan of Whimple, sister of the wife of his brother Reginald. Their first son Richard was born in 1920.

H. L. Whiteway took charge of production at Whimple where new hydraulic cyder presses were soon introduced to replace the old screw type. These could exert a steady pressure of 100 tons or more merely by opening a valve. A new generating plant, installed in 1922, piped acetylene gas to all areas of the factory and offices to provide lighting in place of oil lamps. The chemical calcium carbide, when activated by water, was at that time often used for gas lighting on motor car headlamps and bicycles. The 'fishtail' type of burner had a characteristic white flame, unlike the greenish light provided by town gas and incandescent mantles.

Several new motor lorries were now used for local deliveries at both the Devon and London depots. These were not yet fitted with pneumatic tyres and their speed was restricted to 12 miles per hour by regulation. The small Glasgow sales office and store at 63 Washington Street continued to promote business in Scotland and a new manager, John Gollop from Devon, was appointed in April 1924. He was later to become manager of a new and larger depot in Sheffield and remained with the company for more than forty years until he retired in 1963.

"Whiteway's?"
"Yes—Always!"

The drone of the tireless engine—the winding, ribbon road—the glorious sunshine—the warm, sweet air rushing past—the awakening appetite—the green sward—and then the delight of quenching one's thirst with a glass of sparkling Whimple Cyder. ❡ Take Whimple Cyder in *your* luncheon basket. ❡ Whimple Cyders are made solely from the expressed juice of Devon apples. They are incomparably more delicious and healthful than any grape wines, spirits or malted liquors, *yet they cost far less*. ❡ Order to-day of your Wine Merchant, Licensed Grocer or Store, or write direct for Price List B 1 to

**HENRY WHITEWAY & CO., LTD.,**
The Orchards, WHIMPLE, Devon;
or 37, Albert Embankment, LONDON, S.E. 11.

WHITEWAY'S FAMOUS DEVON CYDERS

The main thrust for cyder sales was the Woodbine Blend, a dry cyder that was recommended for those suffering from rheumatism and gout. A circular letter was sent to 23,000 doctors in the United Kingdom during 1922 drawing their attention to this brand of dry cyder. Whiteway's took stands at the Brewers' Exhibition in London and at the Imperial Fruit Exhibition, winning a premier prize for thirty varieties of cyder apples.

# ORCHARD DEVELOPMENT

Cyder apples were now being purchased each autumn from 540 Devon farmers, as well as being harvested from the company's own increasing acreage of orchards. A premium of £1 per ton was paid for Woodbine apples if kept separately. This variety also had the more picturesque name of 'Slack-ma-girdle'.

In the 1920s it was apparent that farmers needed some help and encouragement to plant cyder apple trees and to improve older orchards. Ronald Whiteway continued his father's deep interest in the drive to improve Devon orchards. In 1926, in conjunction with the Devon County Council Agricultural Committee, Whiteway's organised orchard competitions with cash prizes for growers. In December a big meeting was held at The Castle, Exeter, and a committee was formed to consider ways of achieving the desired improvements in the orchards. Henry Whiteway was a member, and his company agreed to give a bonus of ten apple trees for every 100 trees planted before 31 March 1927. This offer was open to all farmers selling apples to cyder makers.

By 1929 the number of local farmers selling apples to Henry Whiteway & Co Ltd had risen to 1,243. Ronald Whiteway instituted an orchard competition for the heaviest yield per acre sold to cyder makers. This scheme was supported by Colin Ross, BSc, agricultural adviser to the Devon County Council. In January 1930 all local farmers and growers were invited to the Whiteway orchards at Whimple for a public demonstration of spraying methods. Machinery was supplied by Drake and Fletcher Ltd, Maidstone, and chemicals by Murphy and Son of Mortlake.

The Devon County Agricultural Committee supported a field day at Knowle Cross orchards, Whimple in May 1932, when the winners of silver cups and prizes received their trophies from the Rt Hon Lord Carrington. It was arranged for an aeroplane to fly over and photograph the proceedings. Various machinery manufacturers demonstrated power sprayers, roto-tillers and other equipment.

The company had been able to purchase a farm in Whimple of 100 acres including a Georgian farmhouse, cottages and outbuildings for £6,000. Soon the fields had been planted with more cyder apple trees. It was only several years later that a water diviner discovered an almost unlimited deep water course on this farm on which a 200ft deep well is still regularly used.

## SALES

A new, bold, and costly advertising campaign was launched in the national press. A full page in the *Daily Mail* on January 1924 cost £1,400. The slogan was '. . . Why take an unknown road? – the Great White-way is before you'. This produced encouraging results and a full page in *The Times* followed on 23 February, and another in colour on the back page of the *Daily Express* in April. This out-of-season advertising for cyder was considered a novelty at that time. Large advertisements followed in the *Scotsman, Glasgow Herald* and *Irish Times*. Unfortunately, 1924 was one of the coldest and wettest summers on record.

The problem of reduced sales in the winter, however, remained and further efforts were made to sell Whiteway's Ginger Wine by offering a 6fl oz flask at 1s 3d (6p). This was supplied at 29 per cent proof spirit and was believed to be superior to that of any competitors. Raisin Wine and Orange Wine were added and a full-page advertisement was booked for 28 November 1927, featuring the 'Dismal Desmond Dog' theme, a soft toy Dalmatian dog being used as a novelty in window displays etc. The price of these wines was 2s 6d (12p) per bottle.

To reinforce the press and advertisements it was decided to send by post a copy of the *Daily Mail* advert to 9,500 licensed grocers and wine merchants, together with a ginger wine leaflet

and order card. Further advertisements were placed in the *Daily Express, The Chronicle* and *Daily Sketch*.

In the spring of 1928 many more full-page cyder advertisements were placed in several national papers and a three-month poster campaign in London and county areas commenced in April. Trade customers received further circular letters by post.

Draught cyders, both dry (often called 'rough' cyder in Devon) and medium sweet, were being supplied to ever-increasing numbers of public houses in the southern and western counties. The consistent quality and regular delivery in 6 and 10 gallon oak casks upwards to hogsheads eventually resulted in Whiteway's draught cyders being on sale in the majority of local public houses throughout the south-west. Some landlords, however, preferred to sell it unlabelled.

The spring of 1929 saw an imaginative Cydrax campaign. Half pages and full pages in national dailies were backed up by sending out 75,000 circulars to all unlicensed grocers and 60,000 to cafés and confectioners etc. There were now 350 mineral water firms in the provinces bottling Cydrax under licence and selling it along with their own products. The new slogan for Cydrax was '. . . Cyder's little sister'. Between 1926 and 1932, £250,000 had been spent on advertising.

An important development now occurred in the cyder trade. Hitherto cyders had been generally sold in champagne bottles, elaborately labelled, corked, wired and finished with gold or silver foil. Some half-pints and 'splits' with crown corks were sold in bars, but now 40fl oz beer flagons quickly came into popularity. This large Imperial quart bottle was fitted with a black screw stopper and a simple, paper top strap-label. The effect was perhaps quantity rather than quality. It should be explained that the standard champagne quart bottle was 26⅔fl oz and the half bottle (or pints) was 13⅓fl oz.

The new flagon was sold at 10½d (4½p) plus a returnable deposit of 2d (less than 1p), a lower price than the older brands. Unfortunately, this flagon size, although popular, was less profitable to the company. The wholesalers and retail trade were now being actively supported in many ways besides advertising. Coloured showcards of all sizes for shop windows, attractive menu cards for cafés, glass ashtrays, paper napkins and numerous leaflets and novelties were supplied each season.

Organisations such as the Off-licence Protection Association and Licensed Victuallers' Defence Associations were regularly supported. This usually meant that a well known company in the liquor business would accept an invitation for one of their officials to become president at the Association's annual dinner and dance at a prominent local hotel. Frequently the mayor or other well known dignitaries would attend. Ronald Whiteway, Ronald Henley and Reginald Whiteway took the chair at many of these functions in various parts of the United Kingdom during the 1930s.

## BOTTLING AND PRODUCTION

The volume of cyder sales responded favourably to the marketing initiatives and put pressure on the company to meet the demand. In 1924 a stock of 3,500 oak pipes (120 galls), 10,000 hogsheads (60 galls) and 20,000 bottle crates was recorded. By 1932 there were 5,600 pipes, 3,000 hogsheads and 80,000 bottle crates.

The intervening years had seen the construction at Whimple of several new vat houses by Borsari & Co of Zurich, Switzerland. The Borsari system was developed in the 1870 period as an alternative to the oak vats in general use. Rectangular tanks of reinforced concrete, holding 12,000 gallons or more, were rendered smooth with plaster and lined with glass tiles set in a specially blended wax, impervious to cyder and to wine. Those tanks were built in batches of eight on two levels, and cost 7d (3p) per gallon capacity. In later years many more were constructed, some being of 50,000 gallon capacity. Smaller oak casks of many sizes from 4.5 gallons to barrels (36 gallons) were in use generally for draught cyder and this required the provision of several skilled coopers to repair and maintain the thousands of casks.

The bottling depot and offices in London moved to the larger premises adjoining, at 38–46 Albert Embankment in 1924. New Pontifex bottle-filling machines were installed. These were the 18 head counter-pressure rotary type originally designed for beer.

Semi-automatic labellers were supplied by Purdy Machinery

Company and crown corking machines by Flowers of Wimborne. Corking and wiring machines were usually obtained from France. New carbonating plant and German Seitz sterilising filters were acquired to meet the demand.

The bottling staff, many of them girls from Lambeth and Vauxhall, numbered about twenty-five in 1920, with four in the office. This had risen to 100 by 1923 with eight in the office. The basic rate of pay was £1 4s (£1.20) for a 48-hour week, with foremen and managers receiving from £3 to £4. There was a system of output bonuses from January 1921. This enabled the basic £1 4s (£1.20) to rise to £2 7s (£2.35) for maximum weekly output on a sliding scale.

The Whimple factory and office staff at the same period totalled about seventy people, although some temporary additions were necessary in the apple pressing season.

In the north of England some modest factory premises at Wicker Station were leased from the LMS Railway Company at £125 per annum, and the old Glasgow depot closed. John Gollop came from Scotland to take charge of the new Yorkshire depot. Cyder for bottling was despatched by rail from Whimple in hogsheads to Sheffield. A small bottling and packing plant handled requirements for the north, empties being returned to Sheffield, thereby saving rail freight charges. This depot continued for twenty years until larger premises were found.

# HENLEY AND SONS CYDER COMPANY LIMITED

In October 1930 Ronald Whiteway received a letter from a company broker, H.J. Nathan of London W1, proposing the sale of Henley & Sons Cyder Company Ltd of Newton Abbot, Devon. In recent years that company had not been profitable and directors John and William Henley and Ronald Henley had decided to approach Henry Whiteway & Co Ltd. The negotiations, with many meetings and much correspondence, went on throughout 1931 and 1932, the auditors of both companies having provided details of accounts and a great quantity of comments and advice. Agreement was eventually reached by 17 December 1932, at an inclusive figure of £65,000. The older brothers John and William Henley retired, and Ronald Henley received a six-year contract to manage the Henley branch at Abbotskerswell, Devon, and was made a director of Henry Whiteway & Company Limited. Many of the employees of Henley's remained after the amalgamation, notably Walter Batty in the accounts and Lesley Oaff, a member of the clerical staff who eventually retired after fifty years of service. George Gooding also continued to work in the cellars.

The sales of Henley's cyder continued under the new management, with cost savings being made by integration of accounts' departments and sales organisation. Ronald Whiteway arranged for Lloyds Bank Limited to finance the deal with a loan.

Henry Whiteway, the founder of the firm, died at his home in Exmouth in 1932 at the age of 79. The funeral service was held at St Mary's Church, Whimple, and was attended by members of his family and a large number of employees, customers and local people.

The post-war decade had seen the apples purchased rise from 2,000 tons in 1922 to 9,000 tons, the prices increasing from around £2 to £5 per ton. Salaries and wages had advanced from £3,780 to £25,000 per annum during this period; the sales turnover increased from £70,000, with gross profit £27,000 in 1921 to £460,000 turnover in 1933 and gross profit £212,000; assets had risen to £360,000. Ronald Whiteway, now chairman and managing director, was elected chairman of the National Association of Cider Makers for 1933 to 1934.

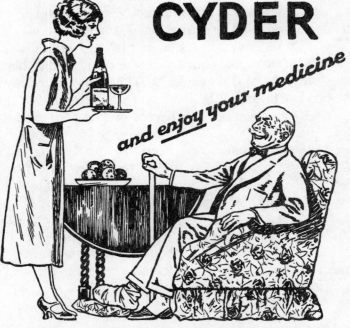

# DRINK
# WHITEWAY'S
# DRY DEVONSHIRE
# CYDER

*and enjoy your medicine*

**FOR** sufferers from RHEUMATIC complaints.

**FOR** ladies who are "SLIMMING."

**FOR** men who are "BEGINNING TO PUT ON WEIGHT."

**FOR** the CONNOISSEUR who appreciates a dry wine.

## 1/- PER SCREW QUART FLAGON

BOTTLE EXTRA AND ALLOWED ON RETURN.

## BOTTLED EXCLUSIVELY AT OUR OWN CELLARS

POMONA DEVONIENSIS

# 6

# Whiteway's Cyder Company Limited and Acquisitions

Early in 1934 serious consideration was given to a proposal to form a public limited liability company to take over from Henry Whiteway & Company Limited, a private company since 1903. Ronald Whiteway began a series of discussions with solicitors Ford Harris and Ford of Exeter, auditors Chalmers Wade of Yeovil, London solicitors Herbert Smith and Company and the registrars Edward de Stein and Company. Counsel was engaged to advise on the project and to give an opinion.

Once the decision had been taken to proceed with the formation of a new public company, much work was needed to prepare the prospectus and draft the memorandum, Articles of Association and contract for sale. By the end of April the details had been agreed. The auditors certified that the average annual profits for the preceding five years were £49,260. The assets of Henry Whiteway & Company Limited were stated as £350,000.

The share capital of the new company was to be £350,000 authorised and issued; 150,000 6 per cent cumulative preference shares of £1 each at 21 shillings (£1.05) per share; 200,000 ordinary shares of £1 each at 25 shillings (£1.25) per share.

Whiteway's Cyder Company Limited was incorporated on 18 May 1934 to acquire as a going concern the old established business of Henry Whiteway & Company Limited on 31 May 1934. The new shares were initially offered to employees and customers only and no applications from the general public were entertained. The issue of shares was heavily over-subscribed and most applicants received less than one third. Several hundred shareholders were registered on the company's books by the completion date, 4 August 1934. The directors were as follows:

Ronald H. C. Whiteway, JP, chairman and managing director
Herbert L. Whiteway, technical director
Reginald P. W. Whiteway, director and London manager
Henry Ford, solicitor
Ronald N. Henley, director and Newton Abbot manager
Secretary, F. Newton
Bankers, Lloyds Bank Limited, Exeter
Auditors, Chalmers, Wade & Company, Yeovil

The ink had scarcely dried on this important document when Ronald Whiteway began negotiations with Schweppes Ltd, Bristol office. This well known company had for a time operated a small cyder factory at Hele in east Devon, situated between the GWR main line and the A38 main road to Exeter. These premises were ideally located in 25 acres of excellent cyder apple orchards. The factory had hydraulic apple presses, oak vats totalling over 300,000 gallons, a good artesian well for water supply and a steam engine with dynamo for 50 volt DC electricity supply. There was a weighbridge for apples and drying equipment for the pomace (apple residue). The land and buildings were valued at £6,000, the plant and machinery at £10,000, together with a manager's house at £210.

Schweppes supplied cyder to a local brewery, Starkey, Knight and Ford, and arrangements were made for Whiteway's to continue deliveries to this firm. The handover took place in July for the sum of £16,310. Whiteway's now had three factories in Devon equipped for pressing apples and fermenting cyder. The employees at Hele, numbering about nine men, were re-employed at their familiar jobs under Mr A. Robins, manager.

The next and much larger acquisition took place in the autumn of 1934. At Crabbs Park near Paignton on the south Devon coast was an old established cyder company called N.P. Hunt and Son which had become a subsidiary of H. & G. Simonds, the well known brewers of Reading. Ronald Whiteway heard that possibly the brewery directors would consider disposal of this business and approached Mr F.A. Simonds, one of their directors. Meetings were held in the Savoy Hotel, London, The Junior Carlton Club and other venues. A great deal of amicable correspondence built up whilst the two principals gradually agreed their terms.

This cyder factory consisted of a number of buildings constructed from rough local granite with a large house and cottages, all with fine sea views about a mile inland between Paignton and Brixham, Devon. There was a large number of oak vats ranging from 1,000 gallons to 23,000 gallons with a total capacity of 450,000 gallons, and within the buildings were the usual cyder making plant comprising mills, hydraulic presses, filters, pumps and oil engines. The factory was set in 50 acres of orchard and pasture land, some of which was in demand for housing development. All this was sold to Whiteway's Cyder Co Ltd in December 1934 for £34,000.

A most important part of the contract related to cyder supplies. H. & G. Simonds had used N.P. Hunt's factory for cyder deliveries to all the breweries, public houses and depots which included Reading, Devonport, London, Oxford, Southsea, Woking and Ludgershall, Wiltshire. The brewery now agreed to buy all cyders from Whiteway's exclusively, at special discounts for a period of seven years.

# IMPORTANT ANNOUNCEMENT TO
# MOTORISTS, CYCLISTS
## AND HIKERS

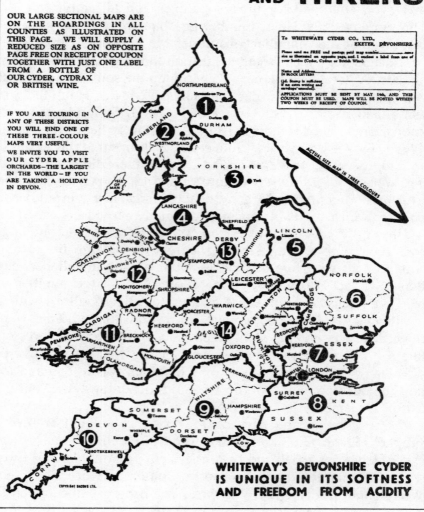

OUR LARGE SECTIONAL MAPS ARE
ON THE HOARDINGS IN ALL
COUNTIES AS ILLUSTRATED ON
THIS PAGE.  WE WILL SUPPLY A
REDUCED SIZE AS ON OPPOSITE
PAGE FREE ON RECEIPT OF COUPON
TOGETHER WITH JUST ONE LABEL
FROM A BOTTLE OF
OUR CYDER, CYDRAX
OR BRITISH WINE.

IF YOU ARE TOURING IN
ANY OF THESE DISTRICTS
YOU WILL FIND ONE OF
THESE THREE-COLOUR
MAPS VERY USEFUL.

WE INVITE YOU TO VISIT
OUR CYDER APPLE
ORCHARDS—THE LARGEST
IN THE WORLD—IF YOU
ARE TAKING A HOLIDAY
IN DEVON.

To WHITEWAYS CYDER CO., LTD.,
EXETER, DEVONSHIRE.

Please send me FREE and postage paid map number............name
also as illustrated on opposite page, and I enclose a label from one of
your bottles (Cyder, Cydrax or British Wine).

Name and Address
IN BLOCK LETTERS

(A Stamp is sufficient
if no extra writing and
envelope unsealed).

APPLICATIONS MUST BE SENT BY MAY 14th, AND THIS
COUPON MUST BE USED.  MAPS WILL BE POSTED WITHIN
TWO WEEKS OF RECEIPT OF COUPON.

ACTUAL SIZE MAP IN THREE COLOURS

WHITEWAY'S DEVONSHIRE CYDER
IS UNIQUE IN ITS SOFTNESS
AND FREEDOM FROM ACIDITY

# WHITEWAYS

## PUT

# CYDER AND CYDRAX REGD.
### (Non-Alcoholic)

## "ON THE MAP"
## AS NATIONAL BEVERAGES

**WHITEWAY'S DEVONSHIRE CYDER** is the ideal beverage for motorists, cyclists and hikers. It is of comparatively low alcoholic strength and can therefore be enjoyed freely as a regular, refreshing drink when "on the road."

**WHITEWAY'S CYDRAX** (non-alcoholic) is aptly described as "Cyder's Little Sister," and is prepared from Whiteway's Devonshire Cyder. It is of medium sweetness, with the soft, thirst-quenching sub-acidity of the apple and its delightful sparkling character—so full of bubbling life—makes it the perfect beverage for young people and abstainers.

| | | | | | |
|---|---|---|---|---|---|
| **CYDER MEDIUM-SWEET** IN SCREW QUART FLAGONS | | | | **10½d.** | (IN SOME LOCAL COUNTIES 10½d.)<br>(IN SCOTLAND & N. IRELAND 1/-) |
| **CYDER DRY** | " | " | " | " | **1/-** (EVERYWHERE) |
| **CYDRAX** (NON-ALCOHOLIC) | " | " | " | " | **9d.** (EVERYWHERE) |

SPECIAL PRICES IN EIRE AND IN FOREIGN COUNTRIES.

## ALWAYS KEEP A FLAGON IN THE CAR OR KNAPSACK

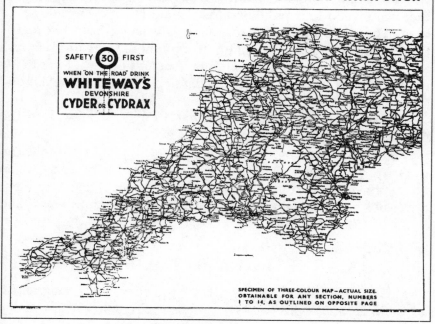

SAFETY **30** FIRST
WHEN "ON THE ROAD" DRINK
**WHITEWAYS**
DEVONSHIRE
**CYDER** OR **CYDRAX**

SPECIMEN OF THREE-COLOUR MAP—ACTUAL SIZE.
OBTAINABLE FOR ANY SECTION, NUMBERS
1 TO 14, AS OUTLINED ON OPPOSITE PAGE

The trade marks and labels of N.P. Hunt were assigned to Whiteway's. Some fifty of Hunt's former customers were also expected to be supplied in future by Whiteway's. These included several well known hotels in London: The Berkeley, New Claridges, The Savoy, Simpsons and the breweries Hall and Woodhouse; Ind, Coope and Allsopp; Strong and Company; Ushers Wiltshire Brewery; Whitbread's and the armed forces NAAFI. This acquisition increased the sales of Whiteway's cyder by nearly half a million gallons annually.

In February 1935 discussions on yet another possible purchase were in progress. This was E. Hill & Sons Limited of Staverton, near Totnes in south Devon, whose premises were approachable only by narrow country lanes, and the GWR branch line to Ashburton. The premises, known as Hillcroft, occupied a four acre site of various stores and cellars containing some forty oak vats totalling 340,000 gallons, and 1,000 pipes (120 gallons). There were four apple presses and mills, filters, a steam engine and other equipment. On the site were eight old cottages and the firm owned four public houses selling Hill's cyder and some beer. These were let to tenants at rents ranging from £32 to £65 per annum. Hill's also supplied fifty public houses in Plymouth and south Devon with a few in Somerset and Dorset. Eventually the sale was agreed for £39,000, including all buildings, plant and stock of cyder, on 31 March 1935.

The result of these deals was that Ronald Whiteway in the period of a little over two years had acquired four Devonshire cyder firms, thereby increasing his company's production capacity, enlarged cyder storage by nearly double and taken on many more customers, particularly in the Devon draught cyder business carried on in public houses in the south-west and south of England.

# MARKETING AND THE MEDIA

The late 1930s were years of very heavy and imaginative advertising campaigns for Whiteway's cyder, particularly in the spring and summer months, and for the increasingly popular sales of Whiteway's fruit wines, Ruby Wine and British Sherry in the winter. The media used were, as in the past, national dailies, regional papers, trade press and periodicals, poster campaigns on outdoor hoardings, advertisements on buses and at some railway stations. In October 1934 a campaign began whereby eighteen half pages for the wines were inserted each Saturday for six weeks in the *Daily Mail, Daily Express* and *Daily Herald* at a cost of £6,000. This was followed by circulating a copy of the advertisement, price list and order card to all licensed retailers.

The summer of 1935 saw the novel idea of sixteen sheet posters printed with a map for each county and the phrase '. . . Whiteway's Cyder all over Cornwall' or '. . . all over Hampshire' as appropriate. The maps were intended to be useful for motorists and tourists. This was backed up by two full page advertisements and by sending 23,000 circulars to licensed grocers in England and Wales.

In July, Whiteway's had what was believed to be the largest press publicity in one week, as below:

5 insertions 2 pages London daily press
1 insertion 2 pages provincial daily press
3 insertions 2 pages provincial evening papers
1 insertion 2 pages national Sunday papers
2 insertions half pages London daily papers
100 insertions half pages in provincial weekly newspapers

Salesmen's conferences were held twice a year at which each representative was encouraged to give his views and suggestions for improving sales or introducing new packaging or advertising methods. A very large selection of colourful designs for shop showcards, booklets, ashtrays, glass mugs and novelties was always available for retailers and on-licences. The Ideal Homes Exhibition at Olympia in London sponsored by the *Daily Mail*, each March, was regularly used by Whiteway's for promoting Cydrax, 'Cyder's little sister'. A well presented stand in the food hall sold glasses of Cydrax for 2d (0.8p), or quart flagons at 9d (4p). The staff of girls on these exhibition stands worked from 10am to 10pm from Monday to Saturday with only short breaks.

A further heavy press campaign was booked for the following

spring of 1936, when the weather was very bad. Half pages were taken in the *Daily Herald, Daily Mail, Daily Express*, and *Sunday Dispatch*. Circulars were posted to the 48,000 retail grocers in Great Britain.

A similar series of advertisements was repeated the following week. In spite of poor summer weather, Cydrax sales increased by 50 per cent. A team of temporary salesmen for canvassing new Cydrax business was recruited during the summer.

The price of the new screw flagon Devon cyder was 10½d (4½p) and the dry cyder was 1s (5p). The British Wine, which included excise duty, was 2s 6d (12p) for oval quarts and 1s 9d (9p) in bottles. It was the practice of the manufacturers and suppliers to fix retail prices to the public and at that time over-charging or price cutting by retailers was not allowed. The licensed trade in Britain had for many years been divided into two categories. The 'on-trade' consisted of public houses and bars where drinks could be sold for consumption by the customer on the premises. The 'off-trade', on the other hand, comprised licensed grocers, wine and spirit shops and any other premises where alcoholic drinks could only be sold in a container to be taken away. Licences to trade were controlled by magistrates and in the case of on-licences, opening hours were restricted and under police supervision. Licensees and landlords generally were members of their local branch of a Licensed Victuallers' Protection Association, which in turn was supported by brewery companies, distillers and other suppliers of drinks. Whiteway's Cyder Co Limited continued to chair many of their annual banquets throughout the country.

In the spring of 1938 the Whiteway's 'County' maps were again on the poster hoardings all over England and Wales. There were five double page advertisements in the London daily papers, which was believed to be the greatest amount of space ever taken by a cyder manufacturer in one day. During the summer holiday period an aeroplane was hired to tow cyder advertisements along south coast resorts.

The volume of cyder sales had now reached four million gallons per annum which amounted to approximately 25 per cent of the UK commercial cyder market.

# APPLES, WATER AND PLANT

The requirements of the apple orchards and of the hundreds of farmers supplying fruit to the company were not neglected; 15,000 cyder apple trees were given away to farmers in 1934. Challenge cups and cash prizes were awarded for the best improved orchards. The price for apples remained at around £4 per ton throughout the 1930s. The total purchased in 1936 was 16,000 tons, increasing to 18,000 in 1939. The Devon County Agricultural Committee organised an open field day at Seale Hayne Agricultural College, Newton Abbot, Devon, on 7 June 1937. The chairman of the governors, The Rt Hon George Lambert, MP, presented the Whiteway cups and certificates. Another open field day was held at the Long Ashton Research Station, Bristol on 12 May 1938 when Dr S.H. Badcock JP, chairman of the County Orchards Sub Committee presented the Whiteway cups for orchard improvement. In 1939 the last pre-war field day was held at the Whiteway orchards in Whimple on 22 May 1939; on this occasion the prizes were presented by Lt Col G.J. Acland Troyte, DSO, MP.

The increasing volume of cyder produced at Whimple in the 1930s required facilities that a rural village could not easily provide. A reliable water supply was essential for the steam boiler, for washing bottles and casks and for general domestic use. The normal 30ft deep wells were incapable of meeting the demand. In 1926 a well-boring specialist, Isler of London, was engaged to drill an artesian well on the factory site. Water was struck at 1,000ft depth. As pumps could not be used, a long steel pipe was installed, reaching to the bottom and compressed air was applied at the top to force the water up. This supply failed after a few hours and was only replenished a day later.

The next step was to find an experienced water diviner. This was arranged by Plumpton of Cullompton, Devon, a well known well-boring and water engineer. The diviner examined various parts of Whiteway's orchards and eventually struck an unlimited source at Barnshayes, about half a mile from the factory. He predicted that this water would be found at great depth. Boring was commenced and water found at 200ft. At first a small horizontal oil engine was installed which operated a piston pump lowered into the well and supplied 2,000 gallons per hour. In later years an electric submersible pump was installed, capable of delivering 5,000 gallons per hour. This well has never failed in more than fifty years of regular use.

The next requirement was more power to operate various machines for the apple elevators, mills, presses, bottling plant and cyder pumps. Mains electricity did not arrive in Whimple until after 1932, and horizontal oil engines, such as were made by Tangye, Crossley and Blackstone, were found to be suitable. At Whimple a 60hp and, in 1929, a 168hp twin cylinder Tangye were in use. These slow speed, quiet-running engines drove shafting from wide belts, the various sizes of pulley wheels giving the required speed for each machine application.

In the vat houses the old hand-operated semi-rotary pumps were replaced by portable petrol-engined units. The pumps were gear type, made by Flowers of Wimborne, driven by a single-cylinder sleeve-valve engine of 3hp made in Glasgow. These reliable little pumps were capable of delivering 1,000 gallons per hour.

Clarifying or filtering cyder has been a problem for manufacturers since earliest times. The more demanding customers expected bottled cyder or, for that matter, wine or beer, to be bright and free from sediment, however harmless. In the cyder industry filtering plant using paper pulp was sometimes used, or another system using Kieselguhr, a type of special European sand in filter frames, showed varying degrees of reliability. A great advance for the beverage industry arrived when the German Seitz cold sterilising filter came into use in the 1920s. Originally developed for German wine makers, this system used factory-made filter sheets, usually 60cm square and approximately 5mm thick. A substantial iron frame was provided to hold the filter sheets, which were separated by lacquered aluminium plates. The throughput per sheet was about 10 gallons per hour. In practice, a multi-plate frame holding perhaps 100 plates with an output of 1,000 gallons per hour was used. When sterilised by steam, these Seitz filters delivered cyder bright and free from yeast.

A much improved automatic bottle washer developed for the

breweries came on to the market in the 1930s. The problems of cleaning, removing old labels and sterilising several thousand dirty bottles arriving back at the factory every week had been, to say the least, daunting. The Hydro bottle washer, such as made by R. Powley of Sunderland or Dawson Bros of Leeds was a steel cabinet some 20ft long which received the inverted bottles placed on a moving rack, ten or more bottles in a row. As the bottles moved steadily forward into the machinery, jets of warm water rinsed them, followed by jets of caustic detergent at 140°F (60°C), then a section at 180°F (82°C) followed by warm water rinse and then a final cold water jet. The clean, sterile bottles were immediately filled on the rotary fillers. These Hydro washers consumed much steam, water and electric power for the pumps. These machines and other processes meant that more waste water, termed industrial effluent, was generated for disposal. The villages of Whimple and Abbotskerswell (Newton Abbot) had no adequate drainage facilities and small streams soon became polluted as a result. Complaints were sometimes received from farmers downstream where livestock possibly also caused pollution in their turn. Water treatment engineers and biology specialists were engaged in an effort to overcome these problems. The local government authorities certainly did not want to help at that time. At Whimple, a system of large concrete settlement tanks was constructed in which yeast sludge could be removed and acidity regulated before discharge into the stream. The situation was not finally overcome until thirty years later when the Water Authority installed a new main sewer and agreed to accept the company's effluent on payment.

The London depot at Vauxhall had no such problem since adequate mains water, drainage and mains electric power had always been available. This also applied to the small Sheffield depot which was situated in an industrial environment.

## SETTING UP THE NEW WINERY

The steadily increasing sales of the fruit wines, Ruby Wine and British Sherry now justified the fermentation of their British wines by the company instead of buying from outside producers.

The newly purchased factory of N.P. Hunt in Paignton was selected as the future winery in 1935. Mr Olaf, the first wine maker, began to adapt the cyder making plant to wine fermentations. The process required the importation of grape juice, or apricot juice, or others as required from Greece, Cyprus and other Mediterranean countries.

Later, another wine expert, Mr Engelhardt from Germany was engaged to develop the new winery. In 1936, Mr Hallet, a former works manager from the Vauxhall depot went to live at Crabbs Park and was appointed works manager. A new concrete vat house was constructed by Borsari with the new 'Ebon' lining in 1938. This provided 250,000 gallon storage for wines. Mr W.F. Loates was engaged as chemist and remained for many years, becoming winery manager and a director of Whiteway's. The company now had four cyder factories in Devon, the winery at Paignton, and bottling facilities in Whimple, London and Sheffield.

## THE GENATOSAN AGREEMENT

Shortly before the declaration of World War II in 1939, Ronald Whiteway had decided to enter into a license arrangement with Genatosan Limited of Loughborough (the proprietors of the brand 'Sanatogen', a well known tonic food powder) in order to market a new product, Sanatogen Tonic Wine. This was a ruby wine produced by Whiteway's and the sodium glycerophosphate ingredient was supplied by Genatosan Limited. It was to be sold in a champagne shape bottle with distinctive label, foil, and wrapped in amber cellophane, price 3s 9d (19p) per bottle. After the war was over this product became a leading brand of tonic wine and is still sold throughout the United Kingdom and several overseas markets.

## EMPLOYEES

In the 1930s the number of Whiteways' employees averaged about 300. The minimum wage for men was £2 for a 50-hour week, although the average rate in country areas for farm workers was less, about £1 12s (£1.60). There were now about thirty field salesmen in the London and country areas, calling regularly on wholesale and retail customers. Not only did they canvass for orders but they maintained contact with the trade, reported activities and were briefed to introduce Whiteway's new products and advertising matter.

The new cyder depots in Devon were under their former managers: Mr A. Robins at Hele, Mr E. Tucker at Staverton and Mr Ronald Henley at Newton Abbot. In Sheffield Mr John Gollop was in charge, as mentioned, Mr Hallett was general manager at Crabbs Park winery, and in Vauxhall, London, were Reginald Whiteway, Frank Hatley and works manager, Mr Hoskins. There were several loyal staff in the office, Miss Hatley, sister of F.T. Hatley, Miss Wise and Miss Seymour. An office junior Miss L. Rice arrived at this time and stayed with Whiteway's for fifty years until she retired in 1988.

Herbert Whiteway, the technical director, was assisted at Whimple by Mr H. White, works manager. The office and accounts staff at Whimple, who were mostly men, numbered about twenty under chief accountant, Arthur Langman, who held that post for thirty years. Dennis Clapp joined the office in the 1930s and apart from war service remained with Whiteway's for forty-eight years, becoming sales manager and director. Ronald Whiteway was again elected chairman of the National Association of Cider Makers for 1934 to 1935.

The apples pressed in those years had increased considerably and averaged 16,000 tons annually at £4 per ton. In 1939 the sales turnover was £721,000; profits before tax were £94,800 and assets totalled £736,700.

# RESTORES the BALANCE

POMONA DEVONIENSIS

# 7

# World War II

On 3 September 1939, the Prime Minister, Mr Neville Chamberlain informed the British people that they were once more at war with Germany. During the next six years the effects on Whiteway's Cyder Co Limited were traumatic. Normality returned only slowly during the post-war period. The first wartime regulations imposed a blackout of all buildings, street lamps and vehicles after dark. Rationing of petrol, food and clothing soon followed. The military authorities arrived to commandeer all lorries, which caused delivery problems. The initial reaction of customers was to place large orders in a panic move to beat expected shortages. This merely created delivery delays and for a few weeks salesmen were instructed not to travel or take orders. The petrol ration per car for business use was rather less than twenty gallons per month and this meant that rail travel had to be used where possible. The government soon introduced an emergency budget in October which did not tax cyder, but increased duties on British wines by 5d (2p) per gallon. Other taxes caused costs to rise and cyder prices became 11½d (5p) per quart flagon, with Cydrax 10d (4p). Ruby Wine was now 2s 3d (11p) per bottle and Ginger Wine 3s (15p). After this, salesmen were again allowed to resume calling on customers.

Some press advertising was placed in the London daily papers and a poster campaign for Sanatogen Tonic Wine was mounted, with advertisements in 600 provincial papers. A sales conference was held at the Grosvenor Hotel, Victoria, London on 29 December 1939. This was the period described as 'the phoney war', when little seemed to be happening on the war front in Europe, or in the air raids over Britain. In February 1940 a further price increase in Ruby Wine to 2s 6d (12p) per bottle was announced – it was 1s 9d (9p) before the war started. An allowance of 1s 6d (7.5p) per dozen was paid on empty bottles returned.

A new pale dry British Sherry had been in preparation at the winery since 1938, and it was now ready to be placed on the market at a price of 3s (15p) per bottle. In February, 1940, H.P. Bulmer had brought out a competitor for Cydrax under the name Cidona. To counter this threat Whiteway's sent a Cydrax promotion circular to 58,000 grocers in April, and advertising space for cyder and Cydrax was taken when available. By the late summer it had become essential to ration customers to the same quantities they had received in the corresponding month of 1939. The poor apple crop of 1940 was a factor in this. Reginald Whiteway had decided to take a commission in the army and resigned as London director, after which Frank Hatley took over as manager and London director. Some employees left to join the forces or Civil Defence service and this caused production bottlenecks at the works. At the London depot occasional air raid alerts caused loss of output on the bottling lines, but no damage occurred. In the course of 1940 the evacuation of the British Army from Dunkirk and in the autumn the Battle of Britain brought an end to the feeling of a 'phoney war'. By Christmas 1940 orders for all products were pouring in to an embarrassing degree and salesmen were again taken off the road; they were temporarily engaged on clerical work. The price paid for a ton of cyder apples was £6 2s 6d (£6.12) or 50 per cent higher than pre-war. The budget of 1940 had caused a further increase in British wine prices. Ruby Wine rose to 3s (15p) and Sanatogen Tonic Wine to 4s 9d (24p). In January 1941 cyder prices also went up again. A quart flagon became 1s 1d (5½p), and in the spring customers received a quota of only 66 per cent of 1940 deliveries, although draught cyder in cask remained at 100 per cent, with a price increase of 1s (5p) per gallon.

Shortages of paper supplies were also being felt and deliveries of new bottles and crates were becoming uncertain. Customers had to be warned 'no empties, no full goods'. The Ministry of Food controlled the industrial sugar ration, which was based on a percentage of pre-war usage. The grape juice required for the wines was no longer available from the Mediterranean area due to enemy action. Rationed imports were permitted from elsewhere as and when available. By February 1941 the customers' monthly quota of British wines was reduced to 50 per cent of 1940.

More men were being called up for the services and it was becoming doubtful whether the autumn apple pressing could be handled properly. Some local farmers who had a mill and press were asked if they would be able to help by pressing their own and some of their neighbours' apples. In August the government fixed the apple price at £18 13s 4d (£18.66), a significant advance on previous years. The crop was light and Whiteway's were able to buy 7,800 tons.

In October the inevitable price rise followed, quart flagons now being 1s 4d (7p) and Cydrax 1s 1d (5½p). Draught cyders ranged from 4s 4d (22p) to 5s 3d (26p) per gallon.

During the wartime years there was of necessity increasing difficulty in getting spare parts for machinery since most firms had switched to government contract work. Essential supplies of steel, timber and building materials required a licence from the appropriate government department before placing an order. The petrol ration became more restricted; at one period there was no basic ration, and rail freight gave priority to defence

71

needs. Air raids on various towns inevitably caused unpredictable delays to delivery of goods from time to time.

The Whiteway farms, as well as the apple orchards, helped to contribute to the food supply. A dairy herd produced milk and some calves; a flock of sheep, which to a great extent grazed on the orchards, produced lambs and wool; a pig unit producing about 1,000 each year, largely fed on kitchen waste from hotels and army camps, also contributed to the food drive. The mansion known as Whimple House became a training centre for Land Army girls, who were able to learn animal husbandry and other farming skills from the adjoining cattle, sheep and pig operations. Some 200 girls were trained in a year. The Devon War Agricultural Committee received every assistance in this from Ronald Whiteway during the war years.

In 1942 difficulties increased as hostilities extended to the Far East, as well as to the Mediterranean. The budget in April once again imposed sharp increases in duty on British wines of 6s 4d (32p) per gallon. This brought the price of a bottle to 4s 9d (24p). There was no new tax on cyder, however. In order to encourage the return of empty bottles all cyder makers increased deposit charges to 3s (15p) per dozen.

In the autumn, 10,000 tons of apples were bought at £18 13s 4d (£18.66) a ton, the price again fixed by the government. In view of likely rail delays, Whiteway's advised farmers to deliver by road where possible, as many farmers had horses and wagons available.

Towards the end of 1942 the Ministry of Food announced a scheme to economise on the transport of national brands of soft drinks. This meant that Cydrax and many other well known brands could not be sold after 1 January 1943. The Soft Drinks Act divided the country into areas comprising a number of registered local mineral water manufacturers which were only permitted to use the national SDI labels (Soft Drinks Industry) identified only by the registered number, with a designation such as 'ginger ale' or 'soda water'. These were manufactured to the Ministry of Food wartime formulas. Cydrax was not able to be re-introduced for a period of eight years. The budget of April 1943 again raised duty on British wines by 2s 3d (16p)

*Partial Eclipse*

We used to pride ourselves that there was no part of Britain where you could not get Whiteway's Cyder. Now that is changed. Cyder, like many other things, is being zoned to save transport and labour. We can send our cyder only to certain areas, and many people who for years have held Whiteway's in high esteem, must now be denied it until zoning ends.

To the lucky ones in the Whiteway zones we extend our congratulations; to those who must forgo their favourite cyder, we offer our sincere regrets.

**1'6**
PER SCREW
QT. FLAGON
*Bottle Extra*

# WHITEWAY'S CYDER ZONED

per gallon, a bottle of Ruby Wine becoming 5s 6d (27p) and British Sherry 30p.

The next problem to arise was a shortage of materials for the black screw stoppers used on all quart and pint cyder (and beer) bottles. A scheme involving the National Association of Cider Makers was instituted to authorise a quota and issue permits to order supplies. These stoppers were of course washed and re-used many times but there was a regular loss in normal trading.

During those dark days of the war, shortages of labour, materials and transport gradually grew worse, supplies to customers were on quota and there was no prospect of accepting new accounts. Sales representatives were no longer calling on the trade and there was little point in advertising as in pre-war years. Newsprint and paper were in any case restricted.

The cyder apple crop of 1943 was good and the fixed price was reduced to £14 per ton. Farmers were asked to spread their deliveries from early September to late December. Those who could were asked to press the fruit and Whiteway's would buy the juice, for which casks were provided.

In March 1944 the Ministry of Food directed that, in order to reduce demands on transport, a scheme of zoning for the distribution and sale of cyder would be introduced on 1 April. In broad terms Gaymer's of Attleborough could sell in the east coast and Scotland. Bulmer's of Hereford could sell in the Midlands, north-west and Wales. Whiteway's in the south-west and south, London being open to all. The National Association of Cider Makers was given the task of interchanging customers between the zones so that they obtained future supplies from a 'new' cyder maker.

Whiteway's Cyder Company Limited was permitted to sell only in the counties of Cornwall, Devon, Somerset, Dorset and in Wiltshire, Hampshire and south Gloucestershire, and the London area. These regulations applied to bottled and draught cyder. British wines were excluded from zoning rules.

The apple crop was very large, in fact the best since 1939, and the price was again fixed at £14 per ton; 12,000 tons were eventually processed.

It was now found possible to remove the quota on deliveries of cyder, subject to the prompt return of empty bottles and casks. In March 1945 an 'SOS' was circulated explaining that the new bottle supply situation was worse than at any time since 1939. Labels were overprinted with a 'return empties' message.

After the budget, the now familiar price increase was announced for wines. Ruby Wine became 5s 9d (29p) and Sanatogen Tonic Wine 8s 9d (44p) per bottle. The extreme shortage of grape juice resulted in a temporarily lower alcoholic strength of Whiteway's wines from 27 per cent proof spirit to 20 per cent. Customers were allocated only about 30 per cent of their pre-war orders. A 'Labelling of Food' order was published in December requiring most 'intoxicating liquors' to have a declaration of alcoholic strength on the label, together with the kind of fruit, if any, used in the production. Cyder and perry however were excluded from this order.

The war in Europe and the Far East had ended and the long re-adjustment to peace-time conditions began. The cyder zoning regulations were removed in March 1946 and all companies were able to distribute again on a national basis. Hostilities were over but the economic aftermath was to last for several more years. The blackout and air raids had gone, but controls and rationing of food, petrol and most other items continued for some years. The 'sellers' market' did not change overnight due to the considerable delay in obtaining replacements for worn plant, vehicles and timber crates and bottles. A new bottle-washing machine was ordered for the London depot, together with a new set of stainless steel tanks for carbonating cyder, in a new cold room. Orders were again subject to a quota on account of staff shortages and sugar rationing. It was at last possible to import grape juice again from the Mediterranean countries. The British Sherry and Ruby Wine could be restored to the pre-war standards of 27 per cent and 28 per cent proof spirit.

# EMPLOYEES

The frequent increases in cyder prices from 1939 through the war years to the late 1940s were partly due to rising wages arising from the war effort. The agricultural wages that averaged £2 in 1939 to

1940, steadily increased to £3 10s (£3.50) by 1945. The amounts paid to women workers was less, about 50 to 60 per cent of the men's rate. Whiteway's introduced a sick pay scheme in 1943, in which wages were made up to 75 per cent of normal pay for three months, and thereafter according to individual circumstances.

For many years the company had paid pensions to retired employees and widows; these often were about £100 to £200 per annum. In 1946 it was decided to make enquiries about a formal superannuation scheme. After having given consideration to various options a policy was agreed with the Phoenix Assurance Company to provide pensions and other benefits to all regular staff and employees.

Mr H. White retired as works manager at Whimple having served the company for more than thirty years. His assistant, George Benford, who had been with Whiteway's since pre-war times was appointed works manager. Most of those who had served in the Forces had returned to their previous jobs with the company – Dennis Clapp to the office at Whimple, Eddie Coombe, chargehand in the bottling department, Stanley King, salesman, being examples.

In 1946 Richard Whiteway, elder son of Herbert Whiteway, who had served with the Devonshire Regiment and the 6th Airborne Division, joined the company. His first task was to re-start the Export Sales Office which had been unavoidably suspended for six years during hostilities.

Eric Whiteway, son of Reginald Whiteway, and who had been serving in the Indian Army in the Far East, also joined the company in 1947, initially at the London depot in the production and bottling departments. At this time a new farm and orchard manager, John Hales was appointed at Whimple, soon after the disbanding of the Land Army training centre. There was also a change at the winery at Paignton, where Mr Hallet retired and Mr W. F. Loates became the new manager.

In February 1948, W.E. Calow (Bill), for many years engaged in sales in the West End of London, and Richard Whiteway (Dick), joined the board of Whiteway's Cyder Company Limited. Ronald Whiteway was again elected chairman of the National Association of Cider Makers.

Employees in the early post-war years usually went to work by bus, train or bicycle, or in the London or Sheffield depots by tram. In the Devon factories the company owned a number of nearby houses or cottages which were available to employees at low rents. The head office and works at Whimple adjoined the railway station and convenient local services operated between Exeter and stations up the line to Honiton and Axminster, and for this, employees were provided with season tickets. This arrangement continued until the curtailment of rail facilities under Dr Beeching. The total number of staff employed in 1949 was 425. The following year, Mr F. Newton, company secretary, retired after thirty years of service, and Mr C. Reece was appointed in his stead. Eric Whiteway joined the board in the same year.

# TRANSPORT AND FACTORIES

In the war years and after, goods were distributed almost exclusively by rail, empty bottles in crates and casks being returned at an agreed flat rate charge. Railway goods services had, not surprisingly, become run down during the war and nationalisation had caused further uncertainty and lack of competition between the regions (formerly companies).

Consideration was therefore given to the use of company-owned lorries as an alternative. The first batch of four stainless steel 1,800 gallon road tankers on AEC diesel chassis was ordered, to be based at the Abbotskerswell factory, near Newton Abbot. The total cost was £3,500 in 1948. These were used for transporting cyders or wines to the London, Whimple or Sheffield bottling factories. Tankers were a great improvement on the loading of numerous hogsheads into open rail trucks, where damage or loss sometimes resulted.

One drawback at that time was a speed limit of 30mph on lorries with an unladen weight of under 3 tons, and a limit of 20mph for heavier lorries. Diesel engines were still in a minority and lighter trucks of 3- or 4-ton load capacity usually had petrol engines. Whiteway's Cyder Co Ltd used Morris and Guy chassis at Whimple, and Bedford or Austin in the London depot. The pre-war livery of chocolate brown was changed to turquoise cabs, with yellow bodywork, with the company name and products painted boldly on sides and tailboard.

There were, at this period, no motorways and few bypasses. As the lorry fleet gradually built up, use of rail freight declined, and customers received a quicker and more personal service. British Rail, however, still provided a shipside delivery to various docks for export orders.

The small store at the Wicker Station in Sheffield, leased by Whiteway's since 1930, was essentially linked to goods by rail. A search for a larger bottling depot in the city was now put in hand by Ronald Henley and the manager, John Gollop. Eventually a factory building, complete with offices and yard space, was acquired at Savile Street east, Sheffield for £29,000 in 1950. The necessary plant was now ordered including steam boiler, stainless steel tanks, bottle washing machines, bottle fillers, labelling and ancillary equipment. A small fleet of lorries was based at the new premises for customer deliveries in the north of England.

The increasing need for deliveries by road in the Midlands, especially in the Birmingham area, indicated the establishment of a small distribution depot. It was decided that pre-packed cyders and wines should be transported from Whimple by large trunk lorries, and then distributed by smaller vehicles from a Midlands depot. After inspecting various properties, a warehouse, with office and yard was bought at Coventry for £6,250. A manager was engaged with a small warehouse staff and three lorries. This was a time of great activity and prosperity in the motor industry strongholds of Coventry, Wolverhampton and Birmingham, and it soon became apparent that suitable staff were difficult to find and they easily found better paid work in the motor factories.

Meanwhile in Devon, cyder making continued each autumn, 12,000 to 15,000 tons of apples being pressed at the now static rate of £14 per ton. Sugar was still rationed to less than 100 per cent of pre-war purchases, but there were signs that the sellers' market was less strong than for many years. In April 1949 a demonstration of spraying apple orchards took place at Whimple House Farm. Mr Hodell of the National Fruit and Cider Institute from Long Ashton, Bristol and Mr Staplake of the National

Agricultural Advisory Service attended, to advise farmers.

At the company's depot at Hele, Devon, a new tankhouse holding 100,000 gallons was built by Borsari & Co of Zurich, for £13,000 in 1950, and was followed by similar installations at the cyder factory at Abbotskerswell and the winery at Paignton.

A new cyder cooling unit and flagon bottling line was ordered for installation at Whimple.

# SALES – 1945 TO 1950

The re-adjustment to normal trading took much longer than was expected. Sugar was still rationed, petrol was available only on coupons, new cars or lorries were obtained only after many months on a waiting list. Orders for factory plant were similarly on long delivery dates. Worst of all, new bottles were difficult to obtain, and customers were for a time restricted to quotas.

In 1946 the cyder 'zoning' regulations were rescinded and Whiteway's cyders could be sold throughout the United Kingdom again.

In the summer of 1947 the price of bottles of 'Whimple' brand cyder and Woodbine blend increased to 1s 5d (7p), half pints 7d (3p). The Devon cyder in quart flagons was 1s 6d (7p) and draught 5s (25p) per gallon. The salesmen were now back on the road again. The apple crop of 1950 was very large and the price fell to £10 per ton.

Cydrax was re-introduced in November of that year at the price of 1s 3d (6p) per flagon; the advertising announced '. . . Welcome back little Sister'. Originally sold as a non-alcoholic cyder more than forty years before, due to war-time difficulties it had not been available for eight years. The Soft Drink Industry (SDI) scheme had been withdrawn in 1948, enabling branded drinks to be marketed, but sugar rationing and bottle shortages had delayed the return of Cydrax.

Richard Whiteway was now actively getting in touch with the pre-war export agents and customers throughout the world. Merchant shipping was gradually returning to peace-time schedules. The export bottling operations were transferred from the London depot to Whimple. Nearly all overseas orders required

# QUENCHY

# QUESTIONS

Animal, vegetable
or mineral?
*Vegetable.*
Can you eat it?
*No.*
Can you drink it?
*Yes.*
Is it made in any
particular county?
*Yes.*
Is it made in Devon?
*Yes.*
Is it Devonshire Cream?
*No.*
Is it nice and sweet?
*Yes.*
It's cyder!
*Yes.*
Let's have a recap.
It's made in Devon,
it's nice and sweet
and it's cyder . . .
*Yes.*

## Then it must be

# WHITEWAY'S
# CYDER

## MEDIUM—SWEET OR DRY

special labelling or, in any case, non-returnable bottle packs.

In the ten years since 1939 wages had increased by 100 per cent, cyder apple prices by 300 per cent and the cost of other commodities also in varying amounts. The price of flagon cyder, then 10½d (4½p), increased to 1s 6d (7½p) in 1950, and was a modest 55 per cent rise.

The situation with the British wines was dominated by a succession of severe budget excise duty increases. A bottle of Ruby Wine which was 1s 9d (9p) in 1939 had become 7s 9d (39p) in 1947 and was down to 5s 9d (29p) by 1949.

Confusion was caused in November 1947 when differential duty changes on British wine were announced. An increase of 10s (50p) for wines of over 27 per cent proof spirit and 5s (25p) for those under 27 per cent resulted in price changes.

A year later the budget permitted British wines to be fortified with spirit in bond, which had always been the practice with imported ports and sherries. The excise duty in 1939 was 1s 6d (6½p) per gallon and this had risen to 14s 6d (72p) by 1947.

The advertising was being gradually re-started in order to restore public awareness of the brands of cyder, Cydrax and wines. In 1950 the total allocation was £107,000. The principal advertising agents were C. Vernon and Son Ltd of London.

The chairman, Ronald Whiteway, became ill in 1949 and entered hospital for an operation. Although he returned to the office, his health gave cause for concern during 1950 and he died in January 1951 aged 65. A memorial service held at Whimple parish church was attended by more than 300 mourners, including 140 members of staff and employees from the branches in Devon, London and Sheffield.

During his forty-five years in the cyder business, both in Nova Scotia and in Devon, Ronald Whiteway had demonstrated great business acumen and leadership, especially since he became general manager in 1923. The expansion and high reputation of Whiteway's was largely due to his hard work and wise judgement.

His private interests included cricket, which he played as a young man. He became chairman of the Devon Orthopaedic Association in 1941 and gave much support to the Princess Elizabeth Orthopaedic Hospital until it was taken over by the

National Health Service in 1948. The hospital was handed over free of all debt.

Ronald Whiteway also served on the Executive Committee of St Loyes College for the Disabled and as a member of the Council of the Exeter and District Chamber of Commerce. He was for twenty years a magistrate on the Ottery St Mary, Devon bench.

Ronald Whiteway was survived by his widow, Alice. They had no children.

| Year | Sales | Profit before Tax | Assets |
|------|-------|-------------------|--------|
| 1938 | £591,000 | £78,000 | £600,000 |
| 1951 | £2,000,000 | £293,700 | £1,600,000 |

POMONA DEVONIENSIS

# 8

# A New Era

The senior directors were now Herbert Whiteway and Ronald Henley who were appointed joint managing directors – Herbert Whiteway becoming the chairman. Reginald Whiteway was re-elected to the board and moved to Devon in order to attend to business in Whimple.

In April 1951 Cydrax advertising consisted of half pages in the *Daily Express* and *News Chronicle*. In addition, novelty items such as ashtrays and waiter trays were supplied for general publicity. Cardboard, however, was still in short supply for printed showcard material.

For cyder advertising, a poster campaign started in June. Salesmen were eligible for an incentive commission on first orders when new accounts were opened.

The large number of local mineral water manufacturers which traded in every town throughout England and Wales were, in pre-war times, pleased to bottle Cydrax and distribute it in their local areas. The Cydrax was supplied as a concentrated syrup in wooden casks (usually 6 gallons or 10 gallons) together with labels overprinted with the bottler's name and address. This .facility was re-introduced from June 1951.

The cost of the Cydrax and cyder advertising campaigns came to £65,000 and for the British wines and Sanatogen Tonic Wine £67,000, with a further £8,000 allowed for general items.

The responsibilities of the directors were now allocated as follows: Ronald Henley was in charge of the south Devon group, which included the Crabbs Park winery at Paignton and the cyder factories at Abbotskerswell and Staverton. Frank Hatley was in charge of the London office and sales together with W.E. Calow. At Whimple, Reginald Whiteway dealt with the marketing and sales, with Richard Whiteway developing the export department. Eric Whiteway was in charge of production at the Whimple, Sheffield and Hele, Devon factories. Further concrete vats, lined with 'Ebon', a special plastic compound, were built by the Swiss Borsari company at the winery and at the Abbotskerswell cyder factory, and Hele depot.

During 1951 a new drink called 'Babycham', a champagne perry in baby bottles, was gaining popularity in public houses. This was destined to become one of the most successful new products of the post-war era in the drinks trade, and it brought large profits to the manufacturers, Showering Ltd of Shepton Mallet, Somerset.

Meanwhile, Whiteway's made determined efforts to open new accounts in a wide variety of outlets, including hotels, school tuck shops, breweries, bottlers and mineral water firms. At this time cinemas were well supported (television was just starting) and many had popular cafés, which were operated by the Gaumont, Odeon and Associated British Cinemas, and there Cydrax could be sold.

Holiday camps, such as Butlin's, were not forgotten in the drive to sell more Cydrax. A 15-second filmlet was produced using the slogan 'drink more apples the Cydrax way'. The armed

# WHITEWAYS is the word for CHEER!

**Here's a health unto Her Majesty — from the heart of glorious Devon.** Whether *your* Coronation party is a hall-full of people, or a small family group round the radio or T.V., Whiteways can help to make it a real success without undue demands on your pocket. Study the modest prices below, and you will agree that Whiteways is indeed the word for CHEER!

## ..in fact, THREE cheers!

### WHITEWAY'S WINES

Glowing ruby or white. Royal wines for a royal occasion. Wonderful for wine cups. *5/9 per bottle (or large ovals 8/3).* For the sherry lover, Whiteways have a fine Pale Dry British Sherry at 9/6, or a mellow Brown at 5/9.

### WHITEWAY'S CYDER

For 14 reigns the men of Devon have toasted Britain's Kings and Queens in Whiteway's Devon Cyder. Why not join them? *1/8 per screw flagon.* (Extra in Scotland.)

### WHITEWAY'S CYDRAX
REGD.

The younger members of the family can join in the celebrations with this sparkling golden apple drink. Made from Whiteway's Cyder with the same traditional Devon skill. *1/6 per screw flagon.*

services were served by their own organisation, the Navy, Army and Air Force Institute (NAAFI) and there were numerous officers' and NCOs' messes to be approached for trade in cyder and wines.

Caterers to the various agricultural shows were offered special inducements to sell Whiteway's products. Richard Whiteway gave particular attention to the Licensed Victuallers' Association (LVA) by regularly taking the chair at functions throughout the country. As in pre-war years, annual banquets were held in all the larger towns and cities. Suppliers to the liquor trade were pleased to take the chair and provide the customary hospitality as a means of securing business goodwill and for meeting customers on their own territory.

By early 1954 Herbert Whiteway, chairman since 1951, was in poor health, and decided to resign from executive responsibilities, although he remained a director of the company. Reginald Whiteway, the youngest brother, was elected chairman and joint managing director, whilst Ronald Henley remained as joint managing director as before.

# SALES AND NEW PRODUCTS

The company held regional sales conferences in the spring and autumn in four areas – London, Devon, Birmingham and Sheffield. These were semi-formal round table meetings at which the sales representatives were encouraged to discuss any matters with the directors and to put forward their ideas or complaints. The directors were, in turn, able to keep abreast of aspects of trade at grass roots level, which was not always consistent in the different regions.

Advertising was maintained at increasing levels of expenditure in the daily press and trade press, with posters and showcards for retail shops. The advertising agents for Cydrax and British wines were C. Vernon & Sons Ltd, and Dorlands for cyder and Sanatogen Tonic Wine. The total budget in the mid-1950s was £185,000 per annum. It was claimed that 325 million advertisements would appear in a period of six months.

New products were introduced in both the cyder and

British wine markets. A still cyder, known as Devon Inn, in quart flagons, was put on sale for those who did not favour carbonated cyders. Pomona, a strong dry sparkling cyder, packed in a traditional champagne-style bottle, was re-introduced at a price of 5s (25p).

In an attempt to sell British wines to the on-licence trade and in bars, the 3.5fl oz baby bottle was introduced. Ruby Wine and British Sherry were launched to be sold at 1s (5p) in returnable bottles fitted with a new type of easily-removed aluminium cap. Sales of these in the early 1950s became very successful as an all-the-year-round trade.

In view of the evident popularity of Showering's 'Babycham' it was decided to introduce a similar style of sparkling perry in a baby bottle to be called Baby Pom, perry de luxe at 1s 3d (6p). This was put on the market in 1956. Baby Pom was advertised on Radio Luxembourg using a peak listening period at 7pm on Tuesdays, during a record request show. Baby Pom had only limited success and was withdrawn after 1961.

Cydrax, supported by heavy advertising in press and periodicals, was selling very well, but now the competitor known as 'Cidona', produced by H.P. Bulmer, re-appeared on the market. Steps were therefore taken to boost the sales of Cydrax.

1955 was chosen as the year to celebrate the 50-year Jubilee of Cydrax. This took the form of a photographic competition advertised in the national press. Each snapshot entry had to show a bottle of Cydrax. The first prize to the photographer was to be £500, with additional cash prizes totalling £1,000 in all. This competition produced over 3,000 entries by the end of June. A Cydrax Jubilee luncheon was held at the Dorchester Hotel, London, attended by 'Miss Cydrax', directors of Whiteway's and seventeen editors of the trade press. A children's painting competition was also organised in the children's papers – *Eagle*, *Lion* and *Girl* – which received 12,500 entries, the prizes being bicycles. All these activities helped Cydrax to regain its popularity after the war years.

In the autumn an article appeared in the women's section of the *Sunday Mirror* newspaper, advocating cyder vinegar as an aid to slimming. The writer suggested a daily consumption of two teaspoons in a glass of water. This article was not in any way inspired by Whiteway's and the sudden upsurge in demand became embarrassing. Whiteway's had been selling cyder vinegar for more than fifty years, but the demand had been fairly small. Cyder vinegar is made from cyder and its reputed health-giving properties are widely accepted. The company, however, could not use any such claims in advertising material. The price in 1955 was 3s 6d (17p) per pint bottle, and numerous orders continued to arrive at Whimple.

The difficulties in staffing the distribution depot at Coventry made a move necessary. In May 1956, after a further search, new premises were found at Pershore, a country town in Worcestershire. After some initial problems this depot operated very efficiently for ten years under a new manager – David Westcott.

Plans were in hand for an important television advertising campaign for wines in November and December; 15-second 'spots' were booked in London, Birmingham and Manchester, which it was estimated could be seen by more than six million people watching commercial television.

In November an unexpected problem arose following the Egyptian government's decision to take control of the Suez Canal. British and French troops were sent to avert this action and the resulting international crisis caused a sudden petrol shortage, followed by rationing in the United Kingdom. Whiteway's deliveries from Whimple, London, Sheffield and Pershore were now predominantly by road transport and much concern was felt in case the Christmas orders should be affected. The petrol ration for the salesmen was also severely curtailed, being sufficient for only about fifty miles per week, until supplementary coupons were issued. After six months, however, rationing was withdrawn.

In January 1957 a heavy advertising campaign for Sanatogen Tonic was launched in the national daily papers, Sunday papers, various women's magazines and other periodicals such as *Picture Post* and *TV Times*. Commercial TV was used for 13 weeks with 15-second 'spots' in London, Birmingham and Manchester. A satisfactory increase in sales resulted.

The spring campaign for cyder was combined with Cydrax

for the first time, and 30-second TV films in London and the Midlands were supported by the usual press advertisements.

For British wines a special spring wedding advertising campaign started in March with 500 provincial papers featuring the names of their respective towns, eg 'the wedding wine for Penzance'; or for Westmorland, 'Liverpool knows the name for value'.

The prices had been increased slightly – Ruby Wine and British Sherry were 6s 3d (31p), Pale Dry British Sherry 8s (40p). Flagons of Devon Cyder became 1s 10d (9p), with a deposit of 6d (2½p) on the bottle.

For the summer of 1957 a new non-alcoholic drink was introduced under the brand name of 'Peardrax'. This was prepared from pear juice and was a sweet sparkling beverage designed to supplement the long established Cydrax apple drink. Supplied in quart flagons at 1s 8d (8p), the black label featured an attractive pear design. Peardrax was advertised in the *Daily Mirror, Daily Sketch, Reveille* and on Radio Luxembourg. TV spots were booked in London, Midland and northern areas, followed by a special pre-Christmas boost in December.

TV, at this period, was still only black and white, and coloured films were suitable only for cinema advertising. By 1958, commercial TV had been extended to Wales, Scotland and the West of England, and bookings were made on all stations.

The budget of 1958 did not increase duties; in fact there was a small reduction, which enabled some prices to be lowered. Cyder and perry remained duty free.

Whiteway's draught cyders were generally on sale in public houses and bars throughout the south-west and south of England. The familiar oak casks ranged in size from the 4½ gallon, through a range of 6 gallons, 9 gallons, octaves (14 gallons), half barrels (18 gallons), up to barrels (36 gallons) and hogsheads (about 60 gallons), the price being around 5s (25p) per gallon. And a new stoneware jar of 2-gallon size with metal tap and carrying handle was added to this range, primarily for the private consumer.

Sales of the little 3.5fl oz bottles of British Sherry, known as 'splitlets' at 1s (5p), were now well established in licensed bars. Late in 1958 a new brand name and label, Pony Cream British Sherry, was announced at the same price. As with the attractive little animal featured with Showering's Babycham, the opportunities for developing marketing schemes around a little pony were promising, particularly on commercial TV filmlets. The sales of Pony were soon increasing to such an extent that a new 900-dozen-per-hour bottling line had to be ordered to maintain production.

Another new development was to launch Whiteway's cyder in 'tins', known to the trade as cans. Many items of food had been packed in cans since the mid-nineteenth century, especially meat, fish, condensed milk, some fruits, etc.

Since 1946 attempts to produce a satisfactory can for beer had been carried out by the Metal Box Co Ltd in Britain, resulting in cans manufactured from tinned steel sheet and printed with the required label design. The sheets were cut and rolled into tubes and the sides soldered. Plain discs were used for the ends. The interior was lacquered to prevent corrosion of the metal and to protect the flavour of the contents. In the late 1950s Whiteway's approached the Metal Box Co Ltd with a view to supplying a can suitable for sparkling cyder. Experimental batches were filled and kept for 12 months in storage tests before being offered for general sale. A specially-designed filling machine for cans was obtained together with a machine for rolling on the top end discs. Whiteway's first cans had a very striking design in green lacquer, bearing a map of Britain and the brand name 'Export Cyder'. The size chosen was the largest available, 16fl oz, and selling at 1s 5d (7p). One million cans were sold in the first year, 1959 to 1960. Whiteway's Cyder Co Ltd was the first cyder manufacturer to offer sparkling cyder in a can. Advertising was placed in the national daily papers, Sunday papers and specialised periodicals announcing the new development.

# EMPLOYEES

The total employed by Whiteway's Cyder Co Ltd in the mid-1950s averaged 500, of which 185 were at Whimple. The basic rates of pay for farm workers rose from £5 per 48-hour week in

1951 to about £8 10s (£8.50) per 46-hour week in 1961, which brought the annual figure for wages and salaries to £200,000.

A new annual bonus system to be paid to all employees was related to the total distributed to shareholders. A scale of points for weekly pay rates and for years of service enabled amounts ranging from 1½ weeks' to 2½ weeks' pay to be awarded at the time of the Annual General Meeting.

On the retirement of Mr F. Newton, company secretary, Mr C. Reece became secretary and chief accountant. John Gollop, who had been with the company for thirty years, managed the enlarged Sheffield bottling depot. At the winery in Devon, W.F. Loates was manager and wine chemist and John Hales continued as orchard and farm manager until 1957, when he emigrated to Canada. Ian Hardcastle, who had trained at Seale Hayne College in Newton Abbot, was appointed as farms' manager. John Bosch joined Whiteway's in London as senior sales executive; he remained with the company for more than thirty years becoming, in due course, marketing manager and later a director.

Reginald Whiteway, assisted by Dennis Clapp, directed the home sales policies, Richard Whiteway export sales and marketing while Eric Whiteway was in charge of production and transport. Ronald Henley continued to be responsible for the winery at Paignton and the south Devon cyder branches. He was elected chairman of the National Association of Cyder Makers in 1952–53. Ronald Henley's son, Jeremy, joined the company in 1960 at Abbotskerswell.

In November 1959, Herbert Whiteway died at the age of 68, after a long illness. He had served the company for forty-nine years apart from service with the Honourable Artillery Company in 1914–18. Herbert Whiteway had inherited his father's interest in cyder apples and he was an expert in fermenting and blending cyders. He was a somewhat quiet and retiring man, who was greatly respected and liked by all who knew him. The death of his younger son, Sub-Lieutenant E.J. Whiteway, RNVR, in 1945, was a loss which he found hard to bear.

W.E. (Bill) Calow died in 1961 aged seventy. He had been associated with Whiteway's in London for forty years as a special West End accounts' representative, becoming a director in 1949. A man of charm and genial personality, Bill Calow was totally loyal to Henry Whiteway & Co Ltd whose products he promoted in a lifetime of service. Frank Hatley, London director, celebrated fifty years with the company. In Devon, Joe Woodley, cellar foreman and Wilfred Maddocks, cooper, also completed fifty years before retiring. David Westcott became manager of the new Midland depot at Pershore, Worcestershire, in 1968 and was to remain with the company for many years.

It is notable that in the 1950s at least 10 per cent of the workforce had served for more than twenty-five years. These included many from the office, factory, farm, maintenance trades, foremen and management.

In 1957 a firm of business consultants was engaged to review the company strategy. As a result, an up-to-date costing system was installed under a new cost accountant, J.A. Tryon.

Lorry drivers and most of the factory operatives had joined the Transport and General Workers Union, and the company entered into an agreement with that union for the annual negotiations for pay and conditions of service.

|  | 1961 |
| --- | --- |
| Sales | £409,000 |
| Profit before tax | £178,550 |
| Assets | £2,061,000 |

In 1950 the price of the £1 ordinary shares in Whiteway's Cyder Co Ltd had averaged £7 10s (£7.50) on the Stock Exchange and a dividend of 40 per cent was paid.

In September 1957 there was a capitalisation issue with 400,000 shares of £1 (two new shares for each ordinary share held). Ordinary shares were then converted into 5s (25p) stock units. In 1960 these stock units averaged 15s (75p) on the London Stock Exchange, the dividend paid being 13.5 per cent.

Henry Whiteway (1853–1932)

Ronald Whiteway (1885–1951)

Victor Whiteway (1887–1918)

Reginald Whiteway (1895–1978)

Herbert Whiteway (1891–1959)

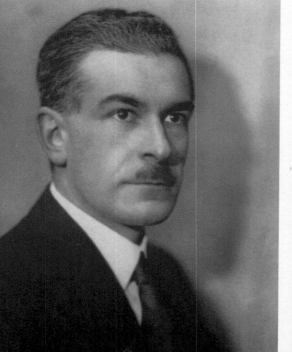

Richard Whiteway (1920–80) with the
Prince of Wales at the Devon County
Show, 1979)

Eric Whiteway (1919– )

A company photograph of 1896. Henry Whiteway stands on the right-hand side of the picture

Horse transport at the entrance of the Whimple factory, 1910

No. 69.

Licensing Act, 1872, s. 74.

Printed by William Pollard & Co.,
North Street, Exeter.

Renewal of License.

COUNTY OF
DEVON
(to wit).

} At the General Annual Licensing Meeting [~~or an Adjournment of the General~~
~~Annual Licensing Meeting~~] holden at *the Town Hall, Ottery St Mary*
on the *twenty second* day of *August* in the year of our
Lord One thousand eight hundred and ninety *nine* for the Division
of *Ottery* in the County of Devon.

We, being *three* of the Justices acting for the said Division, and being
the majority of those at the said Meeting assembled, hereby grant unto

*Henry Whiteway*
of *Whimple* in the said Division and County
~~*Licensed Victualler~~

this renewal license authorising him to apply for and hold any ~~of the~~ Excise License
~~that may be held by a Publican~~ for the sale by Retail at a house situated at

*Whimple aforesaid* known by the sign of
*Cider*
of ~~Intoxicating Liquor~~
*2 Geo 4 and*
to be consumed ~~either on or~~ off the premises. *in pursuance of the Act 1 Wm 4 c 64*
*& Act amending the same*

The owner of the premises in respect of which this License is granted is

*Henry Whiteway*
of *Whimple aforesaid*

This license shall be in force from the *tenth* day of *October 1899*
until the *tenth* day of *October 1900*

Witness our hands

*Coleridge*
*J Kennet Were*
*F B Dickinson*

Signatures of Justices.

* Here insert a licensed victualler, beer house keeper, coffee house keeper, confectioner, eating house keeper, licensed
dealer in spirits, a refreshment house keeper, a wholesale spirit dealer, the holder of a strong beer license, or as the case
may be.

The excise license granted to Henry Whiteway by the magistrates
of Ottery St. Mary, Devon, in 1899

Eric Whiteway inspects the blossom in one of Whiteway's Devon orchards, 1951

(*Overleaf*) Apple harvesting

Joe Woodley, cellar foreman, inspects an early, hand-operated cyder press used by Whiteway's before 1890. This picture was taken in 1953

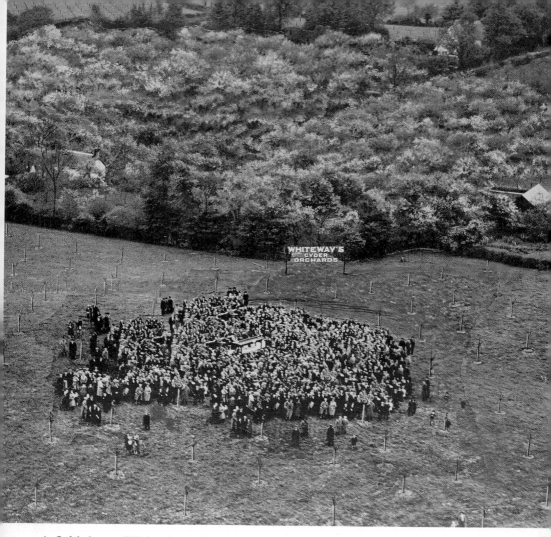

A field day at Whimple, 1932. Cups were presented by the Rt Hon Lord Carrington

Albert Embankment, SE11. Whiteway's horse and motor transport with Reginald and Richard Whiteway in conference with the drivers, 1930

Road tankers at Newton Abbot, 1951. The tanks could carry 1,800 gallons of cyder

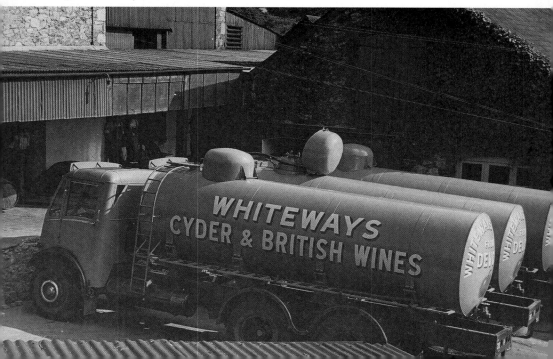

A Morris delivery lorry used by Whiteway's, 1930

All packed up and ready to go! An export order for Baghdad about to leave from Whiteway's Vauxhall factory. Reginald Whiteway stands to the left of works foreman, Mr Potter. The year was 1921

Hydraulic cyder presses. Apple pomace is retained by cloths separated by wooden racks

The Whimple factory of the 1980s. This is the concrete vat house used for cyder fermentation and storage

Repairing casks at the cooper's shop, 1910

POMONA DEVONIENSIS

# 9

# Merger: a New Group

Whiteway's Cyder Co Ltd was not only one of the best known names in the United Kingdom cyder market during more than sixty years, but had become a major producer of British sherries and other alcoholic beverages. At Shepton Mallet, Somerset, Showering's Ltd was an old established firm once renowned for brewing and cyder, but now nationally known for Babycham, the phenomenally successful sparkling perry sold in almost every public house and bar. In 1959 Showering's Ltd had become a public company and had diversified by purchasing R. N. Coate & Co Ltd, the Somerset cyder makers, in 1956. Soon afterwards, in 1961, William Gaymer and Son Ltd of Attleborough, Norfolk, one of Britain's oldest cyder makers, was acquired. Showering's had recently entered the British wine market by buying a small London company, Jules Duval in 1961.

About this time friendly contacts took place at the Great Western Hotel at Paddington Station, between Francis Showering, Ronald Henley of Whiteway's and with a third company in the British wine field, A.D.W. Hunter of Vine Products Ltd, situated at Kingston-on-Thames, Surrey. All three were public companies trading profitably and the intention was to find a way of forming a large new group to trade more effectively in the cyder, perry and British wine businesses. Such an enlarged organisation was expected to be able to rationalise or integrate many of the production and sales activities, and thereby increase profits.

Directors of the three companies held several private meetings to explore the proposals, and their respective firms of auditors were instructed to provide reports on possible terms. The chairman of Showering's Ltd was Herbert Showering, and the managing director, Francis Showering. Vine Products' chairman was Sir Ronald Howe and the managing director was George Roche. Whiteway's chairman was Reginald Whiteway and their joint managing director was Ronald Henley. Showering's auditors were Price, Waterhouse & Co; Vine Products', Mellors Basden & Co; and Whiteway's, Chalmers Wade & Co. It was clear that a new group with capitalisation of about £20 million was to be formed. There was, however, some difference of opinion on the exact split between the three companies. It was agreed that there must be some advantage to shareholders of all the companies, and the financial solution had to be based on what was equitable.

In 1961 the average share valuations were as follows:

| | |
|---|---|
| Showering's Ltd | £9.41 million |
| Vine Products Ltd | £7.90 million |
| Whiteway's Cyder Co Ltd | £1.56 million |

By early September the proposals were in the hands of Derek J. Palmar of Philip Hill, Higginson and Erlangers Ltd and, although discussions had been confidential, rumours were beginning to circulate in the City. The press announcement appeared on 12 September, that an offer of shares in a new holding company – proposed to be called Showering's, Vine Products and Whiteway's Ltd – would be made on the following basis:

| | |
|---|---|
| ***Shares of Showering's*** <br> For every 5 Showering's ordinary shares of 5s (25p) | ***Shares of Holding Company*** <br> 6 ordinary shares of 5s (25p) |
| ***Shares of Vine Products*** <br> For every 100 VP 8 per cent cumulative preference stock units of £1. | ***Shares of Holding Company*** <br> 150 6 per cent cumulative preference shares of £1. |
| For every 5 VP ordinary stock units of 5s (25p) | 7 ordinary shares of 5s (25p) |
| ***Shares of Whiteway's*** <br> For every 100 Whiteway's 6 per cent cumulative preference shares of £1. | ***Shares of Holding Company*** <br> 110 6 per cent cumulative preference shares of £1. |
| For every 20 Whiteway's ordinary stock units of 5s (25p) | 9 ordinary shares of 5s (25p) and £5 in cash. |

The boards of the three companies believed the terms to be fair and reasonable and that the merger was in the best interests of shareholders and employees. The board of the holding company comprised Sir Ronald Howe, chairman, H.M.V. Showering, deputy chairman, F.E. Showering, K.S. Showering, directors of Showering's; A.D.W. Hunter, G.J. Roche, directors of Vine Products; R.P.W. Whiteway and R.N. Henley, directors of Whiteway's.

Each of the companies would continue to trade under its own name and full regard would be paid to the interests of

111

management, staff and employees. A dividend of 17.5 per cent on the ordinary capital for the year ending 31 December 1962 was recommended.

Before the merger the directors of Showering's Ltd owned 70 per cent of the ordinary shares, Whiteway's Cyder Co Ltd owned 42 per cent of the ordinary shares and Vine Products Ltd owned 1.7 per cent of ordinary shares.

The holding company became a public company on 29 September, 1961. The share capital issued was £6 million in 5s (25p) ordinary shares, and £500,000 in 6 per cent cumulative preference shares of £1.

The first secretary was G.T. Wynne-Powell, DFC
Registered office – The Winery, Kingston-on-Thames, Surrey
Auditors – Price Waterhouse & Co, London, EC2
Solicitors – Slaughter & May, London, EC2
Bankers – Lloyds Bank Ltd
Registrars – Philip Hill, Higginson and Erlangers Ltd,
  London, SW1

Later an office was acquired in Curzon Street, Mayfair, London, which provided a boardroom and secretarial offices, at which a new secretary, Eric Seabright, was in charge.

The business activity at Whiteway's continued on the cyder, soft drinks and British wine sectors. Sales of Whiteway's Cyder Royal were increasing especially in the 2-gallon stone jar at a strength of approximately 8 per cent alcohol. It was in competition with Bulmer's Strongbow, Coate's Triple Vintage and Gaymer's Olde English. 1961 advertising was, therefore, concentrated on Cyder Royal.

Cydrax and Peardrax advertising was directed to the provincial evening papers with 11-inch triple-column spaces throughout Great Britain. Children's publications – *Eagle*, *Lion*, and *School Friend* – were used, with some television in the south of England.

Whiteway's cyder had been sold in cans since 1959 and now Peardrax was supplied in a 44cl can for the first time in 1961. In December a heavy press advertising campaign for Sanatogen Tonic Wine was launched with ten insertions in the *Daily Mirror*, eight in the *Daily Herald* and ten in the *Daily Express*. The Sunday newspapers also had a further six advertisements.

Early in 1962 a special half-gallon-size glass pitcher was launched for uncarbonated Cyder Royal and Devon Inn Cyder. This clear glass container had a neat handle and pouring lip incorporated. The price to the consumer was 5s 6d (27p) with returnable deposit on the pitchers.

The budget introduced Purchase Tax at 15 per cent on cyder and soft drinks. This raised the price of cyder quart flagons to 2s 3d (11p) and the 44cl cans of Export Cyder to 1s 7d (8p). A smaller size of can, 33cl, was offered in August 1962 at 1s 3d (6p).

The other companies in this new group selling British wines, Duval, Gaymer's, Magdale, and Vine Products, held meetings to decide on a policy to avoid unnecessary competition with each other. One result was that the Armadillo brand of draught British sherry sold by Whiteway's in small casks was better able to meet outside competition. A new pack in the form of a flexible 5-gallon plastic, non-returnable container was now available for food use. Although not realised at that time, this meant the gradual demise of the oak casks that had been used for centuries. Most customers preferred a 'throw-away' pack rather than the trouble of returning empty casks.

The baby bottles of British sherry now sold as 'Pony' were to be advertised in the *Daily Express* and *Daily Mirror*, with television in some areas, and on cinema screens. The catchy slogan '. . . Never say neigh to a Pony' was used.

In March 1963 regional sales conferences were arranged in Sheffield, Bristol, London and Exeter, on the same lines as in previous years. The main cyder marketing was concentrated on the new half-gallon pitchers and a quart pitcher using a screw cap.

The packaging of Cydrax and Peardrax in 33cl cans was now beginning and was to become a significant advantage, especially for export. Television advertising for these new products was taken on all stations in short 'spots' of 15 seconds.

The budget of 1964 once again increased excise duty on British wines and resulted in a round of price increases.

At this time the Spanish sherry shippers decided to challenge the use of the word 'sherry' for any wines not produced in the

Jerez region of Spain. This caused the Cyprus, South African and British sherry suppliers to agree on a common policy. Mr Guy Aldous was engaged as Counsel, and evidence was gathered over many months in preparation for the forthcoming case in the Chancery Division of the High Court. The British sherry manufacturers and others sought a declaration that they could continue to sell and advertise British Sherry; Cyprus Sherry; etc.

The judgement, which was not announced until December 1967, granted the continued use of the term British Sherry, Cyprus Sherry and South African Sherry as appropriate. The word 'sherry' alone could be used only for the wine from Spain.

The varying prices of British wines sold by Vine Products Ltd, Magdale Winery and Whiteway's were now reviewed, and early in 1965 a common structure was announced. Bottles were 8s (40p), Sanatogen Tonic Wine 10s (50p) and Pony (baby bottles) 1s 9d (9p). The Armadillo draught became £1 7s 3d (£1.36) per gallon.

## GROUP CYDER ZONING AND RATIONALISATION SCHEMES

The cyder companies in the new group, R.N. Coate & Co Ltd, William Gaymer & Son Ltd, and Whiteway's Cyder Co Ltd, continued to operate independently using their own sales forces and production arrangements. This inevitably led to some competition with each other, rather than with outside manufacturers. In early 1965 a system of zoning for areas of responsibility was introduced in an attempt to overcome internal competition. Whiteway's Cyder Co Ltd was allocated the counties of Cornwall, Devon, Dorset, the Bristol area and Hampshire. Coate's and Gaymer's had the rest of the United Kingdom except for a 'free zone' consisting of London and Northern Ireland. There were seven salesmen in the Whiteway's, nineteen in the Coate's and Gaymer's, and twelve in the free zone. Whiteway's salesmen continued to sell Cydrax, British wines and Pony British Sherry all over the country.

The following spring a similar rationalisation move took place for Pony Cream British Sherry which was primarily sold in on-licensed premises. The Whiteway's sales force was principally organised to deal with off-licenced stores, and the Showering's Ltd sales organisation was mainly engaged in selling Babycham and Britvic fruit juices to the on-licensed public house trade. It was arranged that in future, whilst the Whiteway's winery would continue to produce the Cream British Sherry, the selling would be transferred to Showering's Ltd. At the time Pony was probably the only British sherry to be available to the bar trade.

Later in 1966 the recurring problem of inter-company competition between the sales departments of Vine Products Ltd and Whiteway's brought about a carefully worked out rationalisation of product type. In this, Vine Products Ltd took responsibility for all branded bottled British sherries and those bottled under customers own labels, also large orders in casks or tanker loads.

Whiteway's became responsible for áll branded bottled fruit wines, all draught wines in small containers and Sanatogen Tonic Wine.

At this time an important new change in legislation made it illegal for manufacturers to fix selling prices to the public. This amounted to the abolition of resale price maintenance (RPM) and meant that only a recommended, and not a fixed, sale price could be used in advertising or price lists. Consequently any item could vary considerably from shop to shop, and the supermarkets, now beginning to open in the larger towns, took full advantage of this.

The consumer price of Cydrax and Peardrax quart flagons was 2s 2d (11p), recommended, and the 33cl cans 1s 2d (6p) in 1968.

After a regular series of budget increases the British wines had risen to about 11s (5p) and Sanatogen Tonic Wine to 12s (60p). The advertising of all products continued at increasing levels in the press and television, a total of £330,000 per annum being allocated in the mid-1960s. The agents were C. Vernon & Sons, and Hedley Byrne.

In May 1968, some changes were made in the organisation of group cyder sales. A new company called Coate's, Gaymer's and Whiteway's Ltd was established to handle the marketing, sales and accounts for the whole country. An exception was the West Country (Devon, Cornwall, Dorset, the Bristol area and

Hampshire), in which area Whiteway's continued to handle the sales of all the group cyders.

## DIRECTORS AND STAFF

The new group of companies provided for an interchange of directors as a means of liaison between subsidiary companies. Francis Showering and A.D.W. Hunter of Vine Products Ltd joined the board of Whiteway's Cyder Co Ltd in April 1962.

At the winery in Paignton a new chief chemist, Alister Macrae (BSc, Edin) was engaged. On the sales side T.N. (Tommy) Gray joined as special representative to look after the larger brewery customers. A new cost accountant, E.J. (Ted) Webb came to Whimple following the departure of J.A. Tryon in that department. In later years Ted Webb moved to the group headquarters at Shepton Mallet, becoming managing director of Showering's Ltd and also a member of the Whiteway's board.

The Sheffield bottling depot closed in February 1963 and the distribution was transferred to a group depot at Huddersfield. John Gollop, the manager, retired after a long career with Whiteways of more than forty years.

In 1964 Mr A.D.W. Hunter resigned from the Whiteway's board and Mr E.D. Clapp was appointed. In December Ronald Henley, who had spent a lifetime in the cyder business, originally with Henley & Sons Ltd, decided to retire, and Richard Whiteway was appointed to the board of Showering's, Vine Products & Whiteway's Ltd in his place, and he also became chairman of the National Association of Cyder Makers in 1964–65. Sadly, Ronald Henley died suddenly quite soon after his retirement.

Norman Townsend who had joined Whiteway's ten years previously became works manager at Whimple. Frank Hatley who had first gone to Henry Whiteway & Co Ltd in 1911 at Vauxhall, retired as London director in April, 1965. Peter Mann, who had been with a well known brewery, joined the company as production manager and assistant to Eric Whiteway at Whimple.

In order to reduce overheads and improve profits, the Vauxhall depot, used by Whiteway's since 1901, was closed in 1965 and the premises sold for a sum in excess of £110,000. The

London office was transferred to another location used by the group at Syon Lane, Isleworth, where John Bosch, marketing manager, retained an office. Bottling and distribution was increased at Whimple where a new automatic flagon bottling line was installed at a cost of £33,500. The old Henley's cyder factory at Abbotskerswell, Devon, was also closed, partly on account of insoluble difficulties with the Water Authority and drainage problems. Some of the employees at these two factories transferred to Whimple.

In 1968 the small distribution depot at Pershore was closed and the distribution service and office transferred to a group depot at Rubery, near Birmingham. The manager, David Westcott, who had been in charge for ten years, took over at Rubery. C. Reece, who had been secretary at Whimple for 18 years, retired in July 1968, E. W. Seabright took over as company secretary at Shepton Mallet, with E. W. Norman as assistant secretary at Whimple.

The basic wage rates payable in the factories at this period were about £15 per week for adult men and £12 for women. Skilled tradesmen and lorry drivers received higher rates. The minimum holidays were about 15 days rising to 20 days for long service.

|             1968              |              |
| ----------------------------- | ------------ |
| Sales                         | 7.9 million  |
| Profit before tax             | £755,000     |
| Assets                        | £3.3 million |

On 20 May 1968, Sir Ronald Howe CVO, MC, the group chairman, announced that Showering's, Vine Products and Whiteway's Ltd, had agreed to a merger with Allied Breweries Ltd. The negotiations had been conducted on a most amicable basis and Keith Showering, Francis Showering, Herbert Showering and Ralph Showering would be joining the board of Allied Breweries Ltd.

POMONA DEVONIENSIS

# 10

# In Pursuit of Exports

The remark 'Exporting is fun' was attributed to a government minister several years ago when trying to encourage industry to improve export performance.

Henry Whiteway & Company were using agents for overseas business as early as 1897. Mr F. E. Johnson of Rock Ferry, Liverpool was engaged to sell on a 10 per cent commission basis. He asked for a special price for cyder exports to Brougham Douglas & Co, Buenos Aires and later particularly requested half-pint bottles as being more easily saleable than quarts. A Mr H. Crankshaw of Leadenhall Street, London, EC replied to an advertisement in *The Times* for an export agent for cyder in

October 1898. He proposed to approach the principal steamship companies for this business. An enquiry about Whiteway's cyder was received from Charles Coate of Bendigo, Victoria, Australia in 1898. Mr A. Stanley Hill of Cape Town, South Africa was also considered as an agent for Cape Province in 1898. In Bombay, India the agents were Phipson & Company, a well known firm to which a consignment was sent in September 1898. This consisted of 18 dozen quarts of Woodbine Blend at 11s (55p) per dozen, and 6 dozen pints at 7s (35p), the order being worth some £200, shipped on ss *Egypt*. In India cyder was sold at 8 rupees per dozen. One of their customers was named as Lt Sykes of Lucknow. An order was sent to Singapore by the Borneo Company Limited of Fenchurch Street, London, EC. They requested a lower price owing to competition from another supplier. The Calcutta agents were B. Smyth & Company Limited, of New China Bazaar Street, with branches in Bombay and London. Richard Levy & Company handled exports to Australia from their London office in Billiter Street, EC.

The general price list of 1904 issued by the new private company, Henry Whiteway & Co Ltd devoted a page to cyder for export. Stocks of fully fermented cyder were kept for direct shipment to hot climates or to agents. Phipson & Co of Bombay wrote '. . . your Cyders have met with great favour here'; and Murray & Co, Karrachee (*sic*) . . . we are very pleased to say your Cyder is considered in India most excellent, and is certainly the best we have ever imported'; Lady Wingate, the Palace, Khartoum wrote '. . . Lady Wingate encloses a cheque in payment of Messrs Whiteway & Co's account and is glad to inform them that the Cyder reached here in excellent condition, and is greatly liked by all.'

At that period champagne quarts or pints were used, being able to withstand high temperatures and rough handling. Bottles were packed in straw sleeves and laid alternately top to bottom in strong wooden cases. During the next decade all price lists included reference to export cyders, and export merchants, shipping agents, import houses, victuallers and caterers were invited to send for particulars, price lists and favourable terms.

The sales increased each year until World War I curtailed

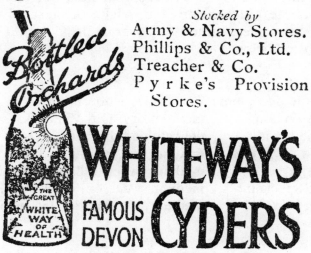

shipping availability. According to a world map in the 1914 price list, Whiteway's shipped cyder to North and South America, the West Indies, West Africa, South Africa, Sudan, the Mediterranean countries, India, Burma, Hong Kong, Japan and Australia. After the war, in 1919, export business was again actively promoted from the London office at Vauxhall.

The Bombay agents were now Herbert, Son & Co, who had stockists in Lahore, Simla, Ferozepur, Jullundur, Umbala, Peshawar and Kasauli. Small advertisements were placed in *The Times of India* in 1919 using the phrase 'The best of drinks for India', giving the names of stockists as Army & Navy stores, Phillips & Co Ltd, and Treacher & Co. Another similar advertisement in the *Civil and Military Gazette* named Herbert, Son & Co, Bombay. These advertisements were repeated throughout this year and in 1920 and 1921. In West Africa the same style of advertisement appeared in *The West African* giving the agents as Crombie Steedman & Co Ltd. A more general advertisement was used in the *Overseas Daily Mail* announcing '. . . Appreciated the world over'. At that period the advertising manager was F.W. Dyer, who dealt with home trade and export advertising matters. The export price list of 1920 contained six sparkling cyders and one still cyder. The standard size case contained three dozen bottles (quarts) or six dozen pints or twelve dozen splits (quarter-bottles), dimensions and weights being supplied for the shipping companies; some were over 112lb (50kg). The cyders were as listed below:

| | |
|---|---|
| Champagne de Pomme | 29s (£1.45) 1 dozen bottles |
| Whimple Pomona | medium dry, Old Vintage 17s (85p) |
| Woodbine blend | delicate and dry 14s (70p) |
| Fair Maid of Devon | medium dry, wine-like flavour 13s (65p) |
| Sweet Alfred | medium sweet, full fruity 14s (70p) |
| Whimple Specialité | medium sweet, or dry 12s (60p) still cyder |
| Exe Valley | medium, a soft cyder 13s (65p) |

Thousands of Fair Maid of Devon Cyder were shipped to

all parts of the world. Its keeping properties were guaranteed in any climate.

A few years later another advertisement appeared in *The Times of India* stating 'Real Devon Cyder now obtainable in India in perfect condition just as you would get it in Devon itself'. The sole agents were Cutler Palmer of Bombay, Calcutta, Colombo, Lahore, Madras, also agents in Karachi, Kashmir, Delhi and Simla.

A new export manager, Ted Wilson was appointed in the 1930s to take charge of all these activities from the Whiteway's London offices. Export bottling was carried out at the London depot on the Albert Embankment SE11 and put on rail to the docks at London, Liverpool or Southampton as instructed. In those days the railway company guaranteed delivery to the docks by the ship's departure date.

A wider range of products was available by the late 1930s for overseas trade. Cydrax was especially suitable for Muslim countries, which often prohibited alcoholic cyders or wines.

The new screw-topped quart flagon bottle supplanted the former champagne-type bottles. Smaller sizes with crown corks were also used. After 1933 the Henley's brands were added to the list in some countries. Whiteway's Ginger Wine, fruit wines, and Ruby Wine were also included, but sales of these were not large in export markets.

These are some of the numerous countries and agents which ordered Whiteway's products in the 1930s:

| | |
|---|---|
| Bahrein | S. Dorabjee & Son |
| Bogota | José Manuel Rodriguez & Co |
| Bombay | Cutler Palmer & Co |
| Buenos Aires | Diggs & Macdevitt Soc anon |
| Buenos Aires | Harrods (Buenos Aires) Ltda (Sidra Champagne) |
| Calcutta | Grierson's Agencies Ltd |
| Cairo | Michael Setton, Son & Co |
| Ceylon | Cargills Limited |
| Malaya | Singapore Cold Storage Limited |

| | |
|---|---|
| Malta | Simonds-Farsons Ltd |
| Meknes | Estab. M. Chapelain and Cie (Cidre Devon) |
| Montevideo | Mateo Brunet SAC |
| Oran | Marce and Cie (also Algiers, Tunis) |
| Panama | Luis Angelini |

The civil war in Spain (which had its own cyder industry) proved to be a temporary advantage for Whiteway's. The South American customers could not obtain their usual supplies from Spain, and Whiteway's quickly took advantage by bottling special cyders with labels in Spanish (Sidra Devon) (Costa Blanca) etc. Every shipment contained suitable advertising material, often in the local language.

The price list for 1937–8 in English, French and Spanish, for example, contained four sparkling cyders and Cydrax, also a selection of Whiteway's British wines. Prices were 'fob' (free on board) at British ports.

Flagon Cyder, medium sweet or dry, 12s (60p) per dozen Imperial quarts (1.13l)

Whimple Cyder, medium sweet, bottles (75cl) 9s (45p) dozen

Whimple Cyder, half bottles (37.8cl) 5s 6d (27p) dozen

Whimple Cyder, quarter bottles (18.9cl) 3s 6d (17p) dozen

Woodbine blend, delicate and dry at 11s (55p) 7s 6d (37p) and 4s 6d (22p) per dozen

Champagne de Pomme, medium dry, 24s (£1.20)

Cydrax, non alcoholic, sparkling bottles (75cl) 9s (45p)

Cydrax, non alcoholic, sparkling half bottles 5s 6d (27p)

Cydrax, non alcoholic, sparkling quarter bottles 3s 6d (17p)

Cydrax, non alcoholic, sparkling Imperial quarts (1.13l) 12s (60p)

The Channel Islands and what was formerly the Irish Free State were also regarded as export territories and their agents placed regular orders. The advent of World War II in 1939 inevitably resulted in the abandonment of the export of non-essential goods, and this trade was not resumed until 1947.

# POST-WAR REVIVAL

Richard Whiteway had joined the company in the sales department in 1947 and began to revive the dormant export business. The first task was to write to all pre-war agents and customers who were still in business. The difficulty in obtaining bottles and wooden cases caused problems on the production side but the government allowed an additional sugar allocation for export orders. In 1948, 26,000 gallons of cyder were sold to twenty-one countries, many of them being British Commonwealth territories, such as British Guiana, Malaya, Gold Coast, Kenya and Trinidad. By 1951 cyder sales had doubled and Cydrax was being sent to several countries, particularly Saudi Arabia, Trinidad and the Persian Gulf. Some success was achieved from 1950 in sending Sanatogen Tonic Wine to Eire and Burma. The cyder sales were at this time 50 per cent of total UK exports of cyder, and for export cyders an advertising budget of about £3,000 per annum was spent.

During the next decade, Whiteway's cyder, Cydrax and wines were despatched to over 100 destinations throughout the world, the total number of gallons increasing steadily, reaching 240,000 cyder and Cydrax, and 18,000 wine in 1960; the export was now controlled entirely from Whimple, and orders were bottled and assembled in the Whimple factory for despatch by rail to the docks. Richard Whiteway ran the export office with only one or two clerical staff and a foreman responsible for packaging and marking for shipment.

In 1957 Roger Gray was engaged as export sales executive. When he left in 1960, Rod Armstrong joined the department and remained for twenty-five years. Another assistant started in the same year; this was Haydn Sully who soon became engaged in export sales and from the 1970s travelled extensively overseas to develop new business.

Importers or agents were appointed in each country and in the main towns of larger areas. The local agent would advise on the regulations, tax system or permits which often dictated what kind of product, alcoholic or non-alcoholic, could be imported. Special labels were usually necessary, either to include details

125

of contents or a translation into the local language. Canada, for example, required both English and French.

In the 1960s business continued to expand and, in 1964, 800 orders for cyder and Cydrax and 350 for various British wines were recorded. The weight despatched in one year was 4,000 tons.

Besides the usual commercial firms, Whiteway's received orders from the British ambassadors at Belgrade, Caracas, Paris and Warsaw, also from British embassies in Moscow and Stockholm, and from high commissioners in Accra and New Zealand.

In Canada all alcoholic liquor was controlled by the Liquor Control Board in each province. This caused difficulties as they were often reluctant to order unless there was a demand and were not co-operative in arranging advertising. Orders for cyders were obtained from the LCB of British Columbia in Vancouver and Victoria, also Edmonton, Alberta, and from Montreal, Quebec and Toronto in Ontario.

The British services established NAAFI agencies where forces were stationed, and Whiteway's cyders, Cydrax and wines were exported to most of these. Examples are: Aden; Belize; Benghazi; Famagusta; Georgetown (British Guiana); Hong Kong; Krefeld (West Germany); Sharjah; Singapore; Takoradi (Ghana); Tobruk; Tripoli; Paris.

Other customers were the Royal Canadian Air Force in Germany, the United Nations Food and Agriculture Organisation in Rome, and Crown agents for East African Railways.

The annual sales of cyder and soft drinks in the early 1970s was about 500,000 gallons, with 70,000 gallons of British wines and Sanatogen Tonic Wines, representing a sales value of over £400,000 pa. In 1971, cyder sales were up 9 per cent, Peardrax and Cydrax sales were up 55 per cent, British wine sales were up 50 per cent, and Sanatogen Tonic Wine sales were up 28 per cent.

The larger countries were not always the most important customers for varying reasons. India and Pakistan did not encourage the import of alcoholic liquors, and had exchange controls. The USA, being a large and prosperous country, naturally attracted the attention of exporters. However, domestic American competition, the US $ at 2.40 to the £ sterling, made the cost of starting new products expensive. Similarly, approaches to the Japanese market were usually disappointing. Europe, including the EEC, was also a very unyielding area having a large range of indigenous cyders and soft drinks.

Many smaller islands became regular importers, however, the most remarkable being Trinidad which was comparatively prosperous among the West Indian Islands, and whose local population bought extraordinary quantities of Peardrax for more than ten years beginning in the 1970s. Peardrax, a sweet sparkling pear drink, evidently suited the local taste and had no serious competition. Supplies of Peardrax and Cydrax were exported from Whimple in quart flagons, 33cl cans and in later years litre bottles and in 25cl cans. The most successful agent was Louis Jay Williams, who became sole importer. Others were Allum Supermarkets; A.L. Pereira; Camacho Bros; Ellen Gillette, Hi-Lo Food Stores; Liong Poi, R. Mohammed & Co, Sang Chong, United Grocers; and Wing Hing. From 1973 the orders totalled 213,575 gallons rising to 800,000 gallons in 1982. This made a total for the years 1973 to 1983 of no less than 5 million gallons. This remarkably successful sales position overshadowed other countries and dominated the Whiteway's sales department at the time.

The West Indies (Caricom area), apart from Trinidad, was beginning to suffer financial difficulties in the 1970s and Sanatogen Tonic Wine, which had enjoyed a good sale, could no longer be exported to the islands. A scheme was investigated whereby the base wine could be fermented in Jamaica and the product manufactured under licence by a local brewery company. A royalty payment was received by Whiteway's for sales in the Caricom area.

By the 1980s some clouds had appeared in the export world. Many of the customers in Africa, and elsewhere, now lived in newly independent states whose economies had run into difficulties. Exchange control and import restrictions followed, which prevented exports of non-essential goods. Alcoholic drinks such as cyder and British wines attracted import taxes or liquor duty which affected sales opportunities. Eventually in Trinidad, Louis J. Williams was forced to consider setting up a local canning factory for soft drinks, including Peardrax, and by 1983 Whiteway's were able to supply the Peardrax as a concentrated extract, although some litre bottles were still imported. Turnover and profit were, of course, seriously reduced as a result.

In 1978–79 the sales of soft drinks and cyder reached a peak of over 1 million gallons per annum throughout the world markets.

Following the death of Richard Whiteway in November 1980, Haydn Sully, who had first joined the company twenty years previously, was appointed export manager. A new assistant, John Casperson, was engaged in 1982 to help in overseas visits to customers.

At this time it was noted that 90 per cent of Whiteway's exports went to ten countries and that 10 per cent went to a further forty-five countries.

In the 1980s numerous new overseas areas were being opened up: Akrotiri, Antilles, Aruba, Ascension Islands, Auckland, New Zealand, Botswana, Brunei, Brussels, Carlingford, Cotonou, Iran, Khartoum, Kuala Belait, Labuan, Limassol, Lisbon, Mina Qaboos, Muttrah, Namur, Nicosia, Norway, Omdurman, Port Elizabeth, Reykjavik, San Francisco, Sweden, Zimbabwe, but exporting was also becoming more difficult. Nevertheless, various countries in the United Arab Emirates were ordering Sanatogen Tonic Wine; an importer in Toronto, Ontario, took eight shipping containers in a year of Cydrax and Peardrax litre bottles, also cans. One of the oldest customers, Cargills of Colombo, Sri Lanka, continued to take litre containers of Whiteway's Devon cyder.

In Jamaica, Sanatogen Tonic Wine was being regularly produced locally using the special extract despatched from Devon. A customer in the Bronx, New York, imported litres of Cydrax and Peardrax; in the USA these soft drinks had to be labelled 'Apple Soda' and 'Pear Soda'. The islands of St Kitts and St Lucia favoured Ginger Wine, Ruby Wine and Sanatogen Tonic Wine, whereas South Africa's agent, C. de Solla, regularly ordered cyder vinegar in bulk 45-gallon drums. The US Virgin Islands purchased litres of Peardrax and Cydrax and small cans.

However, in spite of the above, the foreign currency problem of many countries caused the overall sales of cyder and soft drinks to decline gradually from 700,000 gallons in 1980 to 233,000 in 1986; the wine sales also fell from 34,000 gallons to 19,000.

Since the revival of the export business in 1948, 13.5 million gallons of cyder, Peardrax and Cydrax had been despatched overseas to numerous countries and nearly 1.5 million gallons of British wines. In sterling value terms the most profitable years were from 1977 to 1985 when the annual average sales of exports was £1.9 million.

In 1987 a change was inaugurated. A new company called Showering's International Ltd was given the responsibility for selling all Whiteway's exports, as well as for their sister companies, Showering's Ltd, Goldwell Ltd and the Vine Products' brands. Haydn Sully, for so many years associated with the successful Whiteway's export operation, became a director of Showering's International at Shepton Mallet, thus maintaining the link with Whiteway's exports.

# Fine British Sherry can cost less if you supply the bottle.

Take a bottle along to your local off-licence or licensed grocer and they'll fill it up for you with Armadillo Draught British Sherry.

You'll be pleasantly surprised at the quality. And you'll be even more surprised at the good value you can get this way.

One last thing. There's now a new Pale Cream British Sherry for you to try.

If you're not sure where you can get Armadillo, drop us a line and we'll send you a list of stockists.

## ARMADILLO
DRAUGHT BRITISH SHERRY

Quality British Sherries, Vermouths, Mead and fine British Wines on draught. Whiteways, Whimple, Devon.

# 11

# Allied Breweries: A Time of Change

Allied Breweries, one of Britain's largest brewery groups, had incorporated a number of well known firms which included Ansells of Birmingham, Ind Coope of Burton on Trent, Tetley Walker of Leeds and the Romford Brewery in London, as well as several smaller breweries. Wines, spirits and soft drinks were supplied to their hotels and public houses, and Allied Breweries also owned a large chain of retail off-licence shops, known as Victoria Wine Co Ltd, that operated throughout the United Kingdom. The brands of beer included Double Diamond, Tetley Bitter; Skol Lager and Long Life were also sold in cans.

The Showering's, Vine Products and Whiteway's group became a separate division and operated independently of the beer division. In order to bring the group's accounting year in line with that of Allied Breweries, the year end was moved to the end of September. Whiteway's Cyder Co Ltd continued as before with the same directors. Derrick Holden-Brown, CA, (a director of Allied) had been elected to the board in March 1969 and provided valuable contact with other Allied companies. Reginald Whiteway and Richard Whiteway remained on the board of Showering's Ltd of Shepton Mallet.

The business of marketing the various Whiteway's brands of British wines and Sanatogen Tonic Wine continued, with new products being test marketed. One of these was a light British wine to compete with foreign table wines, but sold in 2-gallon containers, priced at £2.15 per gallon. Small restaurants were encouraged to sell this in carafes or by the glass at about 12p. Cydrax and Peardrax were selling well in quart flagons at 12p and in 33cl cans at 7p. These were advertised on street posters in the early 1970s. A new variety of soft drink was introduced – Cyder Shandy – being a blend of lemonade and cyder. The Whiteway's cyders were now being marketed by Coate's, Gaymer's & Whiteway's Ltd, although the Whiteway's products were still fermented and blended at Whimple. In 1971 Derek Stuart-Todd became managing director of the group cyder company and a number of changes of policy were instituted.

In 1972 an interesting new British wine speciality was announced. This was based on a medium dry British sherry which had been blended with Scotch malt whisky. The price was only 90p per bottle. The label featured a stag's head and the name, Clan Dew, was appropriately Scottish. The new product was advertised in national daily papers and a humorous television film was produced in which the stag's head on a wall appeared to speak.

Whiteway's principal activity was now in the British wines sector and with Cydrax and Peardrax and other soft drinks rather than with cyders which were marketed by a group company.

The company name since 1934, Whiteway's Cyder Co Ltd, was changed to Whiteway's of Whimple Ltd in May 1972, this title being considered less likely to be misleading. Whiteway's continued to be in charge of all export sales of cyder for the group, which business expanded strongly as shown in Chapter 10.

Purchase Tax, which had been applied for many years, was replaced by Value Added Tax (VAT) on 1 April 1973, in order to comply with EEC practice. VAT was levied on the final price of any article (or service) and paid by the consumer, the initial rate being 10 per cent.

The political moves of the Middle Eastern oil-producing countries caused a sudden and drastic increase in all fuel and petrol costs in 1974. For a time petrol supplies were again rationed. At this period there was a serious problem in obtaining adequate supplies of new glass bottles and there was also a shortfall in getting sufficient cans for export and home trade Cydrax and Peardrax. At the time there was virtually only one manufacturer in Britain. Customers were rationed in 1974 and certain sizes of glass bottle had to be imported for British wines.

The budget again raised excise duty which meant an increase of about 10p per bottle. The mid-1970s were noted for serious inflation and various counter-inflation regulations were imposed by the government in an effort to control it.

The soft drinks prices were increased to 18p per flagon, excluding bottle and 33cl cans to 6½p. A Cydrax painting competition for children had received 12,000 entries and many prize winners were announced.

In December it was announced that the chairman of Allied Breweries, Sir Gerald Thorley, was to retire in the new year and that Mr Keith Showering would become a vice chairman; he had been on the board of Whiteway's of Whimple Ltd since 1972, when Derrick Holden-Brown resigned on becoming financial director of Allied Breweries.

The oil and energy crisis caused all companies to take practical steps to conserve fuel and energy. A maximum temperature of 68°F (19°C) was permitted for heating of commercial buildings, the minimum being 60.8°F (17°C). Buildings were to have improved insulation and use of illuminated advertising devices during daylight was restricted. On the roads, new lower speed limits were introduced to conserve petrol or fuel oil.

In 1976 Mr Keith Showering became chairman of Allied Breweries and resigned from the board of Whiteway's. Glyn Davies, divisional chief executive of Showering's, Vine Products and Whiteway's, was elected a director of Whiteway's.

In 1976, the Chancellor of the Exchequer imposed an excise duty on cyder and perry at 30p per gallon. This was the first such duty since the temporary war duty of 1916 to 1923 was levied at 4d per gallon. In the seventeenth century, a cyder excise of one farthing (¼d) per gallon had come into being in 1643. In 1763, the Cyder Bill required tax to be paid at approximately 1d per gallon, but was repealed in 1830.

The demand for canned cyder, Cydrax and Peardrax for both home and export markets was building up steadily. Deliveries were frequently held up by repeated shortages of can supplies and in September 1976 priority was given to export requirements until Christmas. In 1977 a completely new and faster can production line was ordered at a cost of £300,000. This included a specially designed filler, seamer, pasteuriser and packaging machine for applying the shrinkwrap plastic enclosing the trays of two dozen cans ready for despatch.

During this decade inflationary trends were affecting the price of apples as with most other commodities. In 1970 apples were bought at about £12 per ton, in 1975, £30 and by 1980, £57 per ton. These increases, rising labour costs and new excise duty and VAT inevitably increased prices to the consumer.

In 1970 prices were:

| | |
|---|---|
| Cyder – quart flagons | 3s 1d (15.5p) |
| Cydrax – quart flagons | 2s 6d (12.5p) |
| Cydrax – 33cl cans | 1s 4d (6.5p) |

10 years later, in 1980, the corresponding prices were:

| | |
|---|---|
| Cyder – quart flagons | 60p |
| Cyder – 44cl cans | 22p |
| Cydrax – quart flagons | 43p |
| Cydrax – 33cl cans | 14p |

The British wine prices had also increased, due to annual duty increases, VAT and general inflation. Per bottle prices were as follows:

| | |
|---|---|
| Whiteway's Fruit Wines | £1.70 |
| Clan Dew, blended with whisky | £1.77 |
| Sanatogen Tonic Wine | £1.80 |

The British sherries sold on draught were over £6 per gallon.

In April 1978, Mr Reginald Whiteway, chairman of Whiteway's of Whimple Ltd for twenty-four years, died after a short illness. Mr Reg, as he was known, was the youngest son of Henry Whiteway, the founder of the company. The funeral at the Parish Church, Whimple, was attended by a large congregation of employees, colleagues and directors of Allied Breweries.

Reginald had first gone into the business in 1913 and, apart from army service in 1914 to '18 and again in World War II, he spent most of his working life with the company in London or at Whimple. He saw Whiteway's grow to one of the major companies in the wine and spirit division of the giant Allied Breweries group. During his time as head of Whiteway's, the profits (before tax) rose from £127,400 to £1.5 million and the assets from £1.7 million to £10 million.

Richard Whiteway was appointed chairman of Whiteway's of Whimple Ltd and joint managing director with Eric Whiteway.

In August 1978 it was announced that the boards of Allied Breweries Ltd and J Lyons & Co Ltd had reached an agreement whereby Allied would make an offer for the whole of the ordinary share capital of Lyons. In due course Allied Breweries changed its name to Allied-Lyons, the Lyons' businesses of tea, coffee, ice cream, cakes and catering becoming a new division.

Early in 1979 there was a wave of strikes involving transport drivers and this began to affect export orders to the docks and delivery of materials to the factories.

Dennis Clapp, who had joined the company in 1930, retired as sales director, although he remained on the board in a non-executive capacity. Peter Garratt, who for some years had been a regional sales manager, became home sales manager and Haydn Sully became export sales manager.

The pressure of export sales required a larger order assembly and despatch department. Most orders were now sent in containers for direct transit to the docks and ship. A new warehouse at Whimple was erected at a cost of £78,000. A building adjoining Whimple railway station was bought from British Rail and converted into a new administration block including board room, reception and car park, export offices and catering facilities. This amounted to £75,000 and it was opened in September 1980.

During the next month Richard Whiteway visited export customers in the West Indies and USA, and following his return to Heathrow Airport, he was tragically killed in a motor accident while driving home to the West Country.

Richard Whiteway joined the company in 1946 at Whimple and began the task of re-starting the export business, the remarkable success of which is told in Chapter 10. Two years later he became a director of Whiteway's Cyder Co Ltd and chairman in 1978. He also served on the boards of Showering's Ltd, Vine Products Ltd and on the divisional board at Shepton Mallet. Richard Whiteway was again elected as chairman of the National Association of Cider Makers for the year 1969–70. He was well known in the South West for his great interest in cricket and, in particular, the Whimple and Whiteway's Cricket Club. He also supported hockey and squash which he continued to play for many years.

At the funeral service over 350 people filled the church at Whimple – employees, friends, directors of Allied-Lyons and representatives of many sporting clubs. He was survived by his widow, five sons and one daughter.

## DIRECTORS AND STAFF CHANGES

In 1970 Peter Mann left and John Poulter, from Allied Breweries at Burton on Trent, became production manager at Whimple. The assistant secretary, Mr E.W. Norman, died after a long illness, in February, and Peter Rosewell took over as chief accountant and assistant secretary. A new cost accountant,

R.J. Jordan, was engaged and Derek Lascelles also joined the main office as financial accountant and office general manager. In 1972 Ray Jordan transferred to another group company and Chris Bradford became the new cost accountant. In September 1973 Peter Rosewell moved to Shepton Mallet as divisional financial accountant. Derek Lascelles was then promoted to chief accountant and assistant company secretary at Whimple; Mike Bull being appointed assistant financial accountant.

At the Crabbs Park winery, Paignton, Ken Parkinson was engaged as assistant chemist and at Whimple Nick Pring joined the laboratory staff on the cyder and soft drinks side.

In 1976 John Poulter left and Derek Lascelles was chosen to succeed him as production manager, relinquishing his duties as assistant secretary to Chris Bradford.

Following the retirement of Mr W.F. Loates, who had served continuously at the Paignton winery since 1935, and as manager for more than thirty years, his assistant Alister Macrae took over as manager in May 1977.

In the late 1970s Mike Sennitt was financial accountant and Alan Klinger management accountant, Haydn Sully remaining in charge of export.

Norman Townsend, works manager, retired after twenty-three years' service and Bob Slocombe was appointed in his place. Jack Delaney transferred to the Hele branch as depot manager.

There were a number of board changes during the decade. In 1970 the directors were R.P.W. Whiteway (chairman), Richard Whiteway, Eric Whiteway, Dennis Clapp, Francis Showering and Derrick Holden-Brown, CA.

In 1972 Derrick Holden-Brown resigned on being appointed financial director at Allied Breweries, and Keith Showering was elected. In 1975 he resigned and Ted Webb, a director of Showering's Ltd was appointed. Later Glyn Davies, the divisional chief executive, was elected to the Whiteway's board. Sadly, he died suddenly the following year. In 1977 John Bosch, marketing manager, and W.F. Loates, winery manager were elected. On the death of Reginald Whiteway in 1978, Richard Whiteway became chairman and joint managing director. In December 1980, after Richard's tragic death, Eric Whiteway

137

was appointed chairman and managing director and three new directors were elected – Chris Bradford, finance director and assistant company secretary; Peter Garratt, sales director; and Derek Lascelles, production director. John Bosch remained as marketing director. The non-executive members were Dennis Clapp, Francis Showering and Ted Webb.

The number of employees at that time was 350, including production, transport, clerical, sales and other staff.

POMONA DEVONIENSIS

# 12

# A Word about Wines

Wine is perhaps as old as mankind; it is referred to frequently in the Bible and was certainly known to the Romans. Wine is the product resulting from the fermentation of grape juice, although wine-like alcoholic drinks have been made for generations from many other fruits such as cherries, raisins, redcurrants etc.

In Britain fermented apple juice is nearly always referred to as a cyder, and pear juice as perry, partly on account of the fact that for many years cyder (and perry) was free of excise duty or tax, whereas wines of all kinds were taxed.

After World War II, cyders and perries of more than 8½° alcohol were regarded as British wines and taxed as such, regardless of the type of fruits used. Some companies sold apple wine at strengths of higher than 8½° alcohol.

*Two of the Best!*

**Cream British Sherry**

**7/6** a bottle

Introduced last year, it proved
an instantaneous success, and is now an
established favourite.

**Rich Golden British Sherry**

**7/6** a bottle

An excellent newcomer to the Whiteway's
wine list, catering for all who prefer
a lighter wine of sherry character.

*Display the new season's showcard,
featuring these wines, for ready sales.*

## Also

WHITEWAY'S BROWN BRITISH SHERRY
**5/9** a bottle
PALE DRY BRITISH SHERRY **7/6** a bottle
RICH RUBY WINE **5/9** a bottle
and SWEET WHITE WINE **5/9** a bottle

# WHITEWAY'S WINES

*—THE RIGHT WINES AT THE RIGHT PRICES!*

WHITEWAYS  WHIMPLE,  DEVON

The reader will note references in this book to British wines, or British sherry, which Henry Whiteway and Company Ltd began to sell in the 1930s. These should not be confused with table wines, which are produced in temperate regions of Europe, the Mediterranean coasts, North and South America, Australia and South Africa. These wines are fermented from fresh grape juice and reach a strength of about 9° to 12° alcohol.

In recent years a number of enthusiastic people have succeeded in cultivating wine grapes in southern areas of England and making good table wines. The volume of these English wines is small compared with European production. Port, sherry, and Madeira wine are in a different category of wine which has been fortified by the addition of brandy to raise the strength to about 20° alcohol.

British wines have been made commercially since the beginning of the twentieth century or earlier, originally by importing raisins or currants which were steeped in water and fermented with yeast and sugar to provide a very palatable alternative to the more expensive imported products. Successive Chancellors of the Exchequer have seen fit regularly to increase excise duties on British wines.

Whiteway's first introduced a ginger wine in the 1920s, followed by Ruby Wine (being an alternative to port) and British Sherry, in the 1930s. The winery at Paignton, Devon, commenced fermentations in 1935. By this time, however, grape juice requirements were fulfilled by Greece or Cyprus in the form of a juice which had been processed in the country of origin to remove much of the natural water content thereby raising the residual sugar, which prevented fermentation during storage or transit to the United Kingdom. At the winery this was re-diluted, a special wine yeast added, and sugar as required to make a strong and sweet British wine of about 15° to 18° alcohol. The usual processes of fining, filtration and maturing took place before being ready for despatch in oak casks for sale, or to the company's bottling depots in Whimple, London or Sheffield.

Several other firms in the United Kingdom were now producing various British sherries and fruit wines, and the National Association of British Wine Producers was formed

to protect manufacturers in fiscal and legislative matters. The largest company was Vine Products of Kingston on Thames.

From time to time, usually following budgets, some change of manufacturing was allowed. One was to permit fortification (ie addition of distilled alcohol) within prescribed limits, as was the practice with port in Portugal, and sherry in Spain. Labelling regulations required the appropriate description such as Apricot Wine, Damson Wine, Ginger Wine etc, to be adopted. The word 'wine' could not be used alone for these products, which were produced in Great Britain.

Following a long civil court case between the Spanish Sherry Association and the British Wine Producers, the ruling, in 1967, allowed the word 'sherry' to be used alone only for the wine from Jerez in Spain. Wines of sherry type originating in other countries such as Cyprus, South Africa or Britain had to be described as British Sherry or Cyprus Sherry, as appropriate, in order to avoid any possible confusion.

In recent years the considerable increase in wine drinking by the British public, particularly of inexpensive white table wines from Germany and Italy, stimulated British wine manufacturers to compete in this growing market.

In the late 1970s Whiteway's wine technologists produced samples of white and red light British wines of 9° alcohol which were to be marketed in the 1980s with considerable success under the brand name Rougemont Castle Light British Wine. The white varieties compare favourably with many of the cheaper imported wines which are sold in supermarkets. Several other firms also now sell similar light British wines.

This is perhaps a long way from the days early in the century when Henry Whiteway thought of some of his finest Devon cyders, 'Apple Sauterne' (still) and 'Pomona Devoniensis' (sparkling) as the 'Wines of England'.

## ROUGEMONT CASTLE

### 1986 PROMOTION ACTIVITY–THE BEST EVER

* £½ million to be spent in selected television areas and on national consumer advertising, including trade press.

* Powerful national consumer promotion, communicated via one million collars and 3 litre box labels. **Super quality free film** with every wine box or two bottles purchased.

* Massive consumer interest and repeat purchase will be generated.

* Further exciting on-pack activity planned for the autumn.

* Complete range of point-of-sale material available.

POMONA DEVONIENSIS

# 13

# Into the 1980s

The early 1980s was a period of modest increases in the sales of most home trade products although some difficulty was appearing in certain export markets on account of currency controls. Several new soft drinks were tested in the market, notably a sparkling apple and honey blend called 'Apple Bee'. Sales however did not develop as hoped and it was later withdrawn. The major supermarkets were now selling a large range of soft drinks at very low prices which did not allow margins for advertising or publicity.

The most important new product in 1981 was the launch of Rougemont Castle. This was a light British wine of 9° alcohol, fermented to resemble the popular medium sweet German table

145

wines. White, red and rosé styles were offered in bottle at the competitive price of £1.48. This was considerably less than the familiar range of Whiteway's fruit wines at £1.90, or the Clan Dew (whisky blend) at £2.02. It should be explained that Rougemont Castle is part of the Norman castle ruins in the city of Exeter. This new light British wine soon became popular and 30,000 cases were sold in the first year.

A new type of pack ideally suited to Rougemont Castle was the 3-litre 'bag-in-box' container, 1983. This idea originated in Australia and consisted of an attractively printed carton containing a special plastic inner bag filled with a reliable press-open tap. A new filling line for this new container was installed at Whimple and it was an immediate success.

In 1983 Rougemont Castle light British wine showed rapid sales increases of 74 per cent for bottles and 125 per cent for the 3-litre boxes. The sales of all other products increased except the Armadillo draught British Sherries, which declined.

Clan Dew was improved by blending with Irish malt whiskey and in addition a medium dry variety was offered for sale.

Rougemont Castle was advertised on TV stations Anglia and TSW from October, and a poster campaign for Armadillo wines used 2,000 sites in November and December. Sanatogen Tonic Wine was advertised in a number of the popular women's weekly magazines.

In the budget of 1984 there was, unusually, a possibility of making a small price reduction for British wines: Sanatogen Tonic Wine now retailed at £2.29, Clan Dew at £2.35, fruit wines at £2.09, Rougemont Castle bottles at £1.55 and a Rougemont Castle 3-litre box now cost £6.15. The Cydrax and Peardrax litres were now priced at approximately 43p and the 33cl cans 20p, with export cyder 44cl cans, 35p.

A new brand of light dry cyder was launched under the name Whiteway's Devonshire Cyder. The 44cl can was designed to resemble a glazed pottery container. A 3-litre bag-in-box also featuring a cyder jar illustration was introduced at the same time.

Meanwhile, experiments were made in the new techniques of using aluminium cans for use with table wines, and when this method had been established, the canning plant at Whimple was able to fill a range of imported table wines for other companies in the wine and spirit division.

On 5 September 1985 it was announced that an Australian firm, Elders IXL, had acquired 6.02 per cent of the ordinary shares of Allied-Lyons plc and might proceed to make a £1.8 billion bid. Elders IXL was a brewery conglomerate and considerably smaller than Allied-Lyons, whose chairman Sir Derrick Holden-Brown immediately rejected the totally inadequate offer and prepared to fight the unwelcome predator. After many months of well planned defence strategy by Allied-Lyons, Elders IXL withdrew and later proceeded to acquire Courage's brewery.

In another major development in April 1986, Allied-Lyons agreed to acquire a controlling interest in a well known Canadian spirits and wine group, Hiram Walker of Walkerville, Ontario. This organisation owned a number of established brands of whisky and other drinks with worldwide sales, and was complementary to the Allied Vintners' wine and spirits division (formerly known as Showering's, Vine Products and Whiteway's) operating in the United Kingdom, and other parts of the world. Subsequently after further integration the name of the division was changed to Hiram Walker-Allied Vintners.

Whilst this was in progress, another merger in the wine and spirits division was announced. Vine Products Limited of Kingston-on-Thames, one of the largest producers of British wines in England, and Whiteway's of Whimple Limited were to merge in June 1986 to form Vine Products and Whiteway's Limited in a move to consolidate the British wine sales and production strategy. The Whiteway's cyder and soft drink activity was at the same time transferred to another group company, Showering's Limited, who were well known for Babycham sparkling perry, and Gaymer's, Old English Cyder and other apple and pear drinks.

Four of Whiteway's directors joined the new board of Vine Products and Whiteway's Limited at Kingston, where the accounting, marketing and sales departments were centralised.

The Whimple factory continued as a production centre for making British wines, cyder, soft drinks and the bottling and canning of various products as in the past.

From 1980 to 1985 Whiteway's of Whimple Limited's annual profits before tax averaged £2 million, the gross assets being £10 million.

## DIRECTORS AND MANAGERS

The Whiteway's board in 1981 consisted of Eric Whiteway, chairman and managing director, J. L. Bosch (marketing), C. D. Bradford (finance), P. Garratt (sales), D. W. Lascelles (production), E. D. Clapp, F. E. Showering and E. J. Webb being non-executive. H. Sully was export department manager, A. J. D. Macrae continued as manager of the Crabbs Park winery, Paignton, and I. F. Hardcastle, farm manager, C. Topham was transport manager, R. J. Slocombe, works manager, assisted by Frank Spencer-Brown and M. W. Sennitt was chief accountant. Malcolm Peaty, an accountant, was seconded from Shepton Mallet as personal assistant to Eric Whiteway.

Sir Keith Showering, chairman of Allied-Lyons plc died suddenly in 1982 and was succeeded by Sir Derrick Holden-Brown, CA.

In March 1983 Francis Showering, CBE, resigned from the boards of Whiteway's and other companies in the Allied group. It was largely as a result of his great business ability that 'Babycham' became a national drink from the 1950s, and he was the instigator of negotiations which led to the original Showering's, Vine Products and Whiteway's Limited merger in 1961. Michael Jackaman, MA, a director of Allied became chairman of Showering's, Vine Products and Whiteway's Limited and joined the Whiteway's board in April.

Eric Seabright, for twenty years secretary of all the divisional companies, died suddenly in December 1983. He was succeeded by Martin Howard ACIS who had been a member of the secretariat for some years at Shepton Mallet.

In 1984, Eric Whiteway, the chairman and managing director, reached the age of sixty-five and a new managing director, R.C. Grunberg, was appointed from September. Robert Grunberg had for several years been general manager of William Gaymer & Sons at Attleborough, another company in the wine and spirit division.

For many years annual negotiations had been conducted with officials of the Transport and General Workers Union and company shop stewards in an atmosphere of give and take on both sides. In 1980 the basic rate in the factories was £68 for a 40-hour week, rising to £98 for skilled grades. Emphasis was placed on several productivity changes. Further increases followed in 1981 and a 7 per cent rise in 1982.

In 1983 holidays were a minimum 20 days rising to 25 days for long service. The pay scales were £81 rising to £126, and agreement reached in 1984 for a 39½ hour week which started in January. The next year wages rose by 5½ per cent when a 39-hour week was put into operation. In 1986 a 38-hour,

4½-day week was introduced, the factory closing at midday on Friday. Wages now ranged from £96 to £149, reflecting increases of over 30 per cent since 1980.

The board of Allied-Lyons had for some years paid a special bonus to all regular employees based on group profits. This in some years resulted in two weeks' pay being distributed in December.

In February 1985, E.J. Webb retired from Whiteway's board and E.B. Colwell, a director of Allied-Lyons, was elected in June and H. Sully, the export manager in September.

Rod Armstrong, export department executive for twenty-five years, retired and a new marketing manager, Austin McRoberts, joined the company at Whimple. Robert Grunberg left in August and Derek Lascelles took over as general manager, Eric Whiteway remaining as chairman.

The merger of Vine Products and Whiteway's of Whimple Limited in June 1986 resulted in further organisational changes and this is therefore a convenient point to conclude the history of Whiteway's of Whimple.

# Epilogue

In May 1986 Allied-Lyons announced the acquisition of a controlling interest in Hiram Walker Spirits of Walkerville, Ontario, Canada. This company owned many well known brands of whisky and other spirits which were well established in Canada, the United States and Europe.

The company known as Showering's, Vine Products and Whiteway's Ltd, originally formed in 1961, had since 1968 been the wine and spirit division of Allied-Lyons plc. In 1986 the company was renamed Allied Vintners, the chairman and chief executive being Mr Michael Jackaman, with its headquarters at Shepton Mallet, Somerset. Almost at the same time the rationalisation of the cyder and British wine business had been announced.

In Chapter 13 it was related that Whiteway's of Whimple Ltd had merged with Vine Products Ltd of Kingston, another company in the wine and spirits division. This company's wine making was expanding at Marston Magna, Somerset, and its head office and original winery (with bottling facilities) were at Kingston, Surrey. A Yorkshire bottling and packing centre at Huddersfield (the former Magdale Winery) looked after distribution in the north. These, in combination with the Whiteway's wineries at Crabbs Park and Whimple in Devon, resulted in an excess of production capacity and this soon led to changes in the operation of the company. Whiteway's of Whimple Ltd became a non-trading company, owning the Whiteway brands, and in 1987, the winery at Paignton closed and production was transferred to Marston Magna, Somerset. Some British wine processing continued at Whimple under Alister Macrae and Ken Parkinson. Nick Pring was appointed general manager in April 1987 and Bob Slocombe remained as works manager.

In March 1988, Allied-Lyons acquired the remaining stock of Hiram Walker. The management boards of Allied Vintners and Hiram Walker were then merged and the administration of the wines and spirits division was divided between Shepton Mallet and Walkerville, Ontario. The large number of product groups, many with world sales, included spirits, liqueurs, light wines and sherry, British wines, several brands of cyder and Babycham perry.

Hiram Walker-Allied Vintners now began to review production and marketing in order to streamline and integrate facilities where benefits could be expected. Whiteway's Whimple factory continued to pack a wide range of British wines, cyders and soft drinks, in bottles and cans for the home and export markets.

In January 1989 a major change in Vine Products and Whiteway's was made public. The management, offices and production were to be re-located at Whitchurch, Bristol, with fermentations continuing in the enlarged winery at Marston Magna, Somerset. The new site was a large modern factory situated south of Bristol and previously used by Harveys, famous for their Bristol Cream Sherry and other wines. The Harveys sherry bottling operations were to be transferred to Spain and the port to Portugal during the early part of 1989. The existing plants of Vine Products and Whiteway's at Huddersfield, Kingston and Whimple were to be run down and eventually closed in the autumn of that year. Then, a new plant and the most up-to-date system of packaging would be installed at Whitchurch, together with some units from the older factories.

Management, office workers and production staff were kept fully informed and opportunities were provided for as many as possible to move to Bristol. For the remainder, generous redundancy terms were provided which, together with a professional job-finding service operating at each location, aimed to help all employees to find new work in their area with the minimum of upheaval and inconvenience.

By August 1989, activities at Whimple had largely ceased,

with only a small number of key personnel remaining to deal with disposals under Peter Garratt, site administrator.

The end of an era for the cyder factory which began in the closing years of the nineteenth century was inevitably regarded with sadness by the many long-serving employees as they moved to new jobs or careers. But the little village of Whimple with its history of 1,000 years can only look forward to more inevitable changes in the twenty-first century.

# Back again!
# WHITEWAY'S
## NON-ALCOHOLIC CYDRAX
RECD

It's good to have Cydrax back again, missed by so many who enjoy a refreshing non-alcoholic beverage. Delicious, sparkling Cydrax is prepared from Whiteway's famous Devon Cyder and contains all the valuable health-giving properties of the apple. It is medium sweet and is the perfect drink for children — they love it — ideal for picnics and for all who enjoy a refreshing temperance drink.

I'M "CYDER'S LITTLE SISTER"

ONLY
## 1/3ᴰ
PER SCREW FLAGON
Bottle extra.

**Prepared from
Whiteway's
Devonshire Cyder**

# APPENDICES

# APPENDIX I
# *Company Directors (1890s–1986)*

*YEAR*                          *DIRECTORS*

**Whiteway & Co**
1890s   Henry Whiteway
1897    Henry Whiteway, Alban Bellairs

**Henry Whiteway & Co Ltd**
1904    H. Whiteway (ch), Ronald H. C. Whiteway, H. Ford,
1920    H. Whiteway (ch), R. H. C. Whiteway, H. L. Whiteway,
        R. P. W. Whiteway

**Whiteway's Cyder Co Ltd**
1934    R. H. C. Whiteway JP (ch), H. L. Whiteway, R. P. W. Whiteway,
        H. Ford, R. N. Henley
1938    R. H. C. Whiteway JP (ch), H. L. Whiteway, R. P. W. Whiteway,
        R. N. Henley
1941    R. H. C. Whiteway JP (ch), H. L. Whiteway, R. N. Henley,
        F. T. Hatley
1949    R. H. C. Whiteway JP (ch), H. L. Whiteway, R. N. Henley,
        F. T. Hatley, W. E. Calow, R. H. Whiteway
1950    R. H. C. Whiteway JP (ch), H. L. Whiteway, R. N. Henley,
        F. T. Hatley, W. E. Calow, R. H. Whiteway, E. V. M. Whiteway
1951    H. L. Whiteway (ch), R. N. Henley, F. T. Hatley, W. E. Calow,
        R. H. Whiteway, E. V. M. Whiteway, R. P. W. Whiteway (January)
1954    R. P. W. Whiteway (ch), R. N. Henley, F. T. Hatley, W. E.
        Calow,

157

*YEAR*                      *DIRECTORS*

**Whiteway's Cyder Co Ltd (cont)**

      R. H. Whiteway, E. V. M. Whiteway, H. L. Whiteway*

1959    R. P. W. Whiteway (ch), R. N. Henley, F. T. Hatley,
        W. E. Calow, R. H. Whiteway, E. V. M. Whiteway

1961    R. P. W. Whiteway (ch), R. N. Henley, F. T. Hatley,
        R. H. Whiteway, E. V. M. Whiteway

1962    R. P. W. Whiteway (ch), R. N. Henley, F. T. Hatley,
        R. H. Whiteway, E. V. M. Whiteway, F. E. Showering*,
        A. D. W. Hunter* (April)

1965    R. P. W. Whiteway (ch), R. H. Whiteway, E. V. M. Whiteway,
        E. D. Clapp, F. E. Showering*, F. T. Hatley*

1969    R. P. W. Whiteway (ch), R. H. Whiteway, E. V. M. Whiteway,
        E. D. Clapp, F. E. Showering*, D. Holden-Brown CA* (March)

**Whiteway's of Whimple Ltd**

1972    R. P. W. Whiteway (ch), R. H. Whiteway, E. V. M. Whiteway,
        E. D. Clapp, F. E. Showering*, K. S. Showering* (January)

1975    R. P. W. Whiteway (ch), R. H. Whiteway, E. V. M. Whiteway,
        E. D. Clapp, F. E. Showering*, K. S. Showering* (to March),
        E. J. Webb* (May), Glyn Davies* (September)

1977    R. P. W. Whiteway (ch), R. H. Whiteway, E. V. M. Whiteway,
        E. D. Clapp, J. L. Bosch, W. F. Loates, F. E. Showering*,
        E. J. Webb*

1978    R. P. W. Whiteway (ch) [died April], R. H. Whiteway (ch June),
        E. V. M. Whiteway, E. D. Clapp, J. L. Bosch, W. F. Loates,
        F. E. Showering*, E. J. Webb*

1980    R. H. Whiteway (ch) [died November], E. V. M. Whiteway
        (ch November), J. L. Bosch, F. E. Showering*, E. J. Webb*,
        W. F. Loates*, E. D. Clapp*

1981    E. V. M. Whiteway (ch), J. L. Bosch, C. D. Bradford, P. Garratt,
        D. W. Lascelles, F. E. Showering*, E. J. Webb*, E. D. Clapp*

1983    E. V. M. Whiteway (ch), J. L. Bosch, C. D. Bradford,
        P. Garratt, D. W. Lascelles, M. C. J. Jackaman MA*
        (April), E. J. Webb*, E. D. Clapp*

1984    E. V. M. Whiteway (ch), J. L. Bosch, C. D. Bradford,
        P. Garratt, D. W. Lascelles, R. C. Grunberg (September),
        M. C. J. Jackaman MA*, E. J. Webb*, E. D. Clapp*

*YEAR*                    *DIRECTORS*

**Whiteway's of Whimple Ltd (cont)**

1985    E. V. M. Whiteway (ch), R. C. Grunberg (to August),
        J. L. Bosch, C. D. Bradford, P. Garratt, D. W. Lascelles,
        M. C. J. Jackaman MA*, E. B. Colwell*, E. D. Clapp*

1986    E. V. M. Whiteway (ch to 23 June), J. L. Bosch,
        C. D. Bradford, P. Garratt, D. W. Lascelles, H. Sully,
        M. C. J. Jackaman MA*, E. B. Colwell*, E. D. Clapp*

* denotes non-executive director.

# Production of cyder in gallons/Price of apples per ton (1898–1980)*

| Year | Gallons | Price | Year | Gallons | Price |
|------|---------|-------|------|---------|-------|
| 1898 | 69,000 | £2.50 | 1923 | 575,000 | £4.25 |
| 1899 | 165,000 | | 1924 | 621,000 | £6.00 |
| 1900 | 253,000 | | 1925 | 805,000 | £6.00 |
| 1901 | 23,000 | | 1926 | 1,035,200 | £5.25 |
| 1902 | 69,000 | | 1927 | 1,715,000 | £3.50 |
| 1903 | 197,800 | | 1928 | 1,955,000 | £4.50 |
| 1904 | 184,000 | | 1929 | 2,300,000 | £4.50 |
| 1905 | 345,000 | | 1930 | 1,380,000 | £5.00 |
| 1906 | 297,000 | £2.50 | 1931 | 3,450,000 | £5.00 |
| 1907 | 230,000 | | 1932 | 2,070,000 | £6.25 |
| 1908 | 358,800 | £1.75 | 1933 | 3,450,000 | £4.50 |
| 1909 | 180,090 | £2.50 | 1934 | 3,680,000 | £4.00 |
| 1910 | 123,750 | | 1935 | 3,724,000 | £4.00 |
| 1911 | 381,800 | £3.00 | 1936 | 3,755,440 | £4.00 |
| 1912 | 299,000 | £1.00 | 1937 | 3,503,100 | £4.00 |
| 1913 | 441,600 | £1.60 | 1938 | 3,249,300 | £4.00 |
| 1914 | 457,700 | £1.25 | 1939 | 3,346,500 | £3.50 |
| 1915 | 290,950 | £1.12 | 1940 | 3,346,500 | £6.12 |
| 1916 | 171,000 | £2.00 | 1941 | 1,795,900 | £18.66 |
| 1917 | 317,400 | £2.75 | 1942 | 2,329,400 | £18.66 |
| 1918 | 26,900 | £20.00 | 1943 | 1,906,200 | £14.00 |
| 1919 | 414,000 | £4.00 | 1944 | 2,771,500 | £14.00 |
| 1920 | 93,500 | £8.00 | 1945 | 2,283,210 | £14.00 |
| 1921 | 419,200 | £2.50 | 1947 | 2,932,500 | £14.00 |
| 1922 | 493,300 | £2.25 | 1949 | 3,113,200 | £14.00 |

| Year | Gallons | Price | Year | Gallons | Price |
|------|---------|-------|------|---------|-------|
| 1950 | 2,407,000 | £10.00 | 1965 | 775,000 | £11.50 |
| 1951 | 2,788,060 | £10.00 | 1966 | 203,000 | £11.50 |
| 1952 | 3,118,850 | £10.00 | 1967 | 552,000 | £12.50 |
| 1953 | 2,043,320 | £10.00 | 1968 | 344,000 | £13.00 |
| 1954 | 1,604,750 | £10.00 | 1969 | 331,200 | £10.00 |
| 1955 | 1,573,200 | £10.00 | 1970 | 816,500 | £13.00 |
| 1956 | 2,501,480 | £10.00 | 1971 | 600,100 | £13.00 |
| 1957 | 2,120,600 | £10.00 | 1972 | 167,900 | £14.00 |
| 1958 | 2,203,780 | £11.00 | 1973 | 176,410 | £25.00 |
| 1959 | 1,930,620 | £11.00 | 1974 | 301,300 | £29.00 |
| 1960 | 1,729,600 | £11.00 | 1975 | 209,300 | £30.00 |
| 1961 | 1,063,750 | £11.00 | 1976 | 391,000 | £35.00 |
| 1962 | 1,651,400 | £11.00 | 1977 | 50,600 | £45.00 |
| 1963 | 1,025,800 | £11.00 | 1978 | 193,510 | £57.00 |
| 1964 | 862,500 | £11.00 | 1980 | 500,940 | £57.00 |

**Author's note:** From 1899 to 1905 and in 1907 and 1910 the exact prices of apples per ton are not known.

# APPENDIX III

## *London Share Prices*
## *(1935–61)*

In 1934, when Whiteway's Cyder Co Ltd was registered, the authorised and issued share capital was £200,000 in ordinary £1 shares and £150,000 in 6 per cent cumulative preference shares of £1.

Below are details of the London Stock Exchange prices from 1935.

| Year | *1935* | *1936* | *1937* | *1938* |
|---|---|---|---|---|
| Highest | 61s 6d | 69s 9d | 75s | 70s 9d |
| Lowest | 48s | 60s 6d | 66s | 56s |
| Div. Paid) | | | | |
| less tax) | 17½ per cent | 17½ | 17½ | 17½ |

| Year | *1939* | *1940* | *1941* | *1942* |
|---|---|---|---|---|
| Highest | 61s | 72s | 68s 6d | 87s 6d |
| Lowest | 55s | 59s | 62s 6d | 66s 6d |
| Div. Paid) | | | | |
| less tax) | 17½ | 17½ | 22½ | 22½ |
| | + 5 per cent | + 5 per cent | | |

| Year | *1943* | *1944* | *1945* | *1946* |
|---|---|---|---|---|
| Highest | £5 3s 1d | £5 6s 0d | £6 5s 0d | £8 8s 2d |
| Lowest | £4 3s 0d | £5 1s 1d | £6 0s 0d | £6 0s 0d |
| Div. Paid) | | | | |
| less tax) | 22½ per cent | 22½ | 25 | 30 |

| Year | *1947* | *1948* | *1949* | *1950* |
|---|---|---|---|---|
| Highest | £9 3s 2d | £9 6s 10d | £9 1s 10d | £8 0s 0d |
| Lowest | £7 2s 6d | £8 5s 0d | £7 2s 5d | £7 0s 0d |
| Div. Paid) | | | | |
| less tax) | 30 + 10 per cent | 40 | 40 | 40 |

| Year | 1951 | 1952 | 1953 | 1954 |
|---|---|---|---|---|
| Highest | £8 1s 5d | £7 15 0d | £5 12s 5d | £7 1s 2d |
| Lowest | £7 15s 0d | £5 0s 0d | £5 0s 0d | £5 8s 5d |
| Div. Paid) | | | | |
| less tax) | 40 per cent | 40 | 40 | 40 |

| Year | 1955 | 1956 | 1957* | 1958 |
|---|---|---|---|---|
| Highest | £6 10s 0d | £5 0s 0d | 8s 7d | 12s 6d |
| Lowest | £4 0s 0d | £3 14s 0d | 8s 7d | 6s 7d |
| Div. Paid) | | | | |
| less tax) | 40 per cent | 40 | 13½ | 13½ |

| Year | 1959 | 1960 | 1961 (to 4 Oct )** |
|---|---|---|---|
| Highest | 19s 10d | £1 0s 2d | 15s 5d |
| Lowest | 11s 2d | 11s 7d | 10s 5d |
| Div. Paid) | | | |
| less tax) | 13½ per cent | 13½ | 13½ (int) |

* In September 1957 a capitalisation issue of shares was announced. Shareholders were offered two new shares for each ordinary share held. These were then converted into stock which was transferable in 5s (25p) units. The company then had a capital of £600,000 in ordinary units of 25p and £150,000 in 6 per cent preference shares of £1.

** In October 1961, 90 per cent of Whiteway's shareholders accepted the proposal to merge with Vine Products Ltd and Showering's Ltd.

163

# APPENDIX IV

# *Advertising Expenditure (1898–1985)*

| Year | (£) | Year | (£) | Year | (£) |
|------|------|------|------|------|------|
| 1898 | 125 | 1930 | 49,355 | 1958 | 206,000 |
| 1899 | 357 | 1931 | 54,575 | 1959 | 289,000 |
| 1900 | 478 | 1932 | 59,527 | 1960 | 294,000 |
| 1904 | 1,175 | 1933 | 65,726 | 1961 | 303,000 |
| 1905 | 1,733 | 1934 | 67,913 | 1962 | 425,000 |
| 1906 | 1,924 | 1935 | 70,686 | 1963 | 323,000 |
| 1907 | 1,680 | 1936 | 70,130 | 1964 | 296,000 |
| 1908 | 2,264 | 1937 | 72,380 | 1965 | 190,000 |
| 1909 | 2,506 | 1938 | 77,543 | 1966 | 225,000 |
| 1910 | 2,577 | 1939 | 106,738 | 1967 | 256,000 |
| 1912 | 2,907 | 1940 | 83,212 | 1968 | 230,000 |
| 1913 | 3,670 | 1941 | 24,260 | 1969 | 238,000 |
| 1914 | 2,706 | 1942 | 24,582 | 1970 | 234,000 |
| 1915 | 1,461 | 1943 | 20,923 | 1971 | 158,100 |
| 1916 | 2,043 | 1944 | 25,482 | 1972 | 219,773 |
| 1917 | 1,322 | 1945 | 41,228 | 1973 | 323,850 |
| 1918 | 1,060 | 1946 | 58,155 | 1974 | 475,646 |
| 1919 | 2,282 | 1947 | 86,347 | 1975 | 471,405 |
| 1920 | 4,717 | 1948 | 79,630 | 1976 | 439,227 |
| 1921 | 6,000 | 1949 | 91,705 | 1977 | 398,162 |
| 1922 | 7,060 | 1950 | 122,580 | 1978 | 366,472 |
| 1923 | 9,750 | 1951 | 153,000 | 1979 | 526,671 |
| 1924 | 14,940 | 1952 | 150,000 | 1980 | 317,133 |
| 1925 | 30,901 | 1953 | 165,600 | 1981 | 322,661 |
| 1926 | 35,574 | 1954 | 177,895 | 1982 | 410,184 |
| 1927 | 49,803 | 1955 | 189,320 | 1983 | 510,586 |
| 1928 | 49,781 | 1956 | 194,475 | 1984 | 628,656 |
| 1929 | 53,090 | 1957 | 205,000 | 1985 | 649,627 |

# APPENDIX V

# *Export Sales (1948–85)*

| Year | Cyder and soft drinks (gallons) | Wines (gallons) | Year | Cyder and soft drinks (gallons) | Wines (gallons) |
|------|------|------|------|------|------|
| 1948 | 26,685 | | 1967 | 219,183 | 52,805 |
| 1949 | 60,379 | | 1968 | 267,521 | 52,653 |
| 1950 | 50,270 | 2,429 | 1969 | 266,955 | 66,500 |
| 1951 | 61,087 | 1,859 | 1970 | 268,395 | 74,890 |
| 1952 | 65,017 | 4,648 | 1971 | 270,409 | 82,122 |
| 1953 | 94,331 | 11,903 | 1972 | 400,240 | 68,226 |
| 1954 | 101,845 | 8,892 | 1973 | 556,887 | 103,719 |
| 1955 | 139,237 | 19,299 | 1974 | 516,386 | 43,934 |
| 1956 | 147,118 | 18,146 | 1975 | 561,782 | 57,253 |
| 1957 | 125,892 | 15,739 | 1976 | 605,864 | 54,112 |
| 1958 | 161,533 | 16,232 | 1977 | 950,523 | 52,555 |
| 1959 | 169,499 | 21,001 | 1978 | 1,014,465 | 39,474 |
| 1960 | 239,614 | 17,818 | 1979 | 1,042,394 | 42,780 |
| 1961 | 288,827 | 28,349 | 1980 | 778,479 | 33,960 |
| 1962 | 193,319 | 33,604 | 1981 | 680,235 | 27,866 |
| 1963 | 228,002 | 33,689 | 1982 | 557,261 | 21,756 |
| 1964 | 227,112 | 43,598 | 1983 | 791,327 | 18,604 |
| 1965 | 216,835 | 43,797 | 1984 | 327,388 | 24,214 |
| 1966 | 214,860 | 39,606 | 1985 | 202,750 | 17,713 |

# APPENDIX VI

## *Destinations for Whiteway's Exports, 1970s*

ANGUILA

ANTARCTICA

ANTIGUA

AUSTRALIA
  Perth

BAHAMAS
  Nassau

BAHRAIN

BARBADOS

BERMUDA

BISSAN

BRITISH HONDURAS
  Belize

BRITISH SOLOMAN ISLANDS

BRITISH VIRGIN ISLANDS

BURMA
  Rangoon

CANADA
  Edmonton, Alberta
  Halifax, N.S.
  Hamilton, Ontario
  Hay River, N.W.T.
  Inuvik
  Manitoba

Montreal
Ottawa, Ontario
Toronto
Victoria, B.C.
Winnipeg
Yellow Knife, N.W.T.

CANARY ISLANDS
  Las Palmas
  Tenerife

COOKS ISLAND

CURACAO

CYPRUS
  Famagusta

DENMARK
  Copenhagen

DOMINICA

EIRE
  Dublin

FALKLAND ISLANDS

FAROES

FIJI

FRANCE
  Paris, British Embassy

GHANA
  Accra

166

GIBRALTAR

GREECE
  Athens

GRENADA

GUYANA

HAITI

HONG KONG

ICELAND

INDIA
  Bombay

INDONESIA
  Djakarta

ISRAEL
  Haifa
  Tiberias

ITALY
  Rome

IVORY COAST

JAMAICA

JAPAN
  Tokyo

KENYA
  Mombasa
  Nairobi

LIBERIA
  Monrovia

LIBYA
  Tripoli

MALAWI
  Blantyre

MALAYA
  Ipoh
  Kuala Lumpur
  Penang

MALAYSIA

MAURITIUS

MONSERRAT

MOROCCO
  Casablanca

NEW GUINEA
  Port Moresby

NEW ZEALAND
  Raretonga
  Wellington

NIGERIA
  Apapa, Lagos
  Ikeja
  Lagos
  Port Harcourt

NORTH YEMEN
  Hodeidah

OMAN
  Muscat
  Salalah

PAKISTAN
  Karachi

PORT LUIS

QATAR
  Doha

REUNION
  Sabah
  Kota Kinabulu

St EUSTATIUS

St HELENA

St KITTS
  Basseterre
  Nevis

St LUCIA

St MAARTEN

St THOMAS

St VINCENT

SARAWAK
Kuching

SAUDI ARABIA
Jeddah
Sierra Leone
Freetown

SINGAPORE

SOLOMAN ISLANDS
Honiara

SOUTH AFRICA
Cape Town
Johannesburg
Natal
Pretoria

SRI LANKA
Colombo

SURINAME
Paramaribo

SWEDEN
Stockholm

THE GAMBIA
Bathurst

TONGA

TRINIDAD
Port of Spain

TURKS ISLANDS

UGANDA

UNITED ARAB REPUBLIC
Abu Dhabi
Dubai
Taiz
Yemen

USA
Grand Canyon
Hartford
Los Angeles
New York

VIRGIN ISLANDS, US

VIRGIN ISLANDS
St Croix
Tortola

WEST GERMANY
Krefeld

ZAMBIA
Kitwe
Lusaka
Ndola

ZEMA

# Bibliography

The following books are in the University of Bristol, Long Ashton Research Station, and can be seen on application to the librarian.

Austen, R.A. *A Treatise of Fruit Trees, also Cider and Perry* (Oxford, 1657)

Carnell, D. *Family Wine Making (Including Cyder Wine)* (London, 1814)

Cooke, C.W. Radcliffe. *A book about Cider and Perry* (London, 1898)

Crochetelle, J. *La Ciderie* (Paris, 1907)

Evelyn, John. *Pomona, an Appendix Concerning Fruit-trees in Relation to Cider* (London, 1670)

Fabius de Champville, G. *Le bon cidre* (Paris, 1896)

Field, George. *A Treatise on the Improved Method of Making Cyder* (Dublin, 1789)

French, R.K. *History and Virtue of Cyder* (London, 1982)

Haines, Richard. *Aphorisms upon the New Way of Improving Cyder or Making Cyder Royal* (London, 1684)

Ham, J. *The Manufacturing of Cider and Perry Reduced to Rules* (London, 1827)

Knight, Thomas Andrew. *A Treatise on the Culture of the Apple and Pear, and on the Manufacture of Cider and Perry* (Ludlow, 1801)

Labounoux, P. et Touchard. *Le Cidre* (Paris, 1903)

Langley, Batty. *Pomona, and a Curious Account of the Most Valuable Cyder Fruit of Devonshire* (Hugh Stafford, London, 1729)

Le Couteur, Francis. *A Treatise on the Cultivation of Apple Trees and the Preparation of Cider* (translation 1813)

Lloyd, F.J. *Reports on Cider Making for Bath and West Southern Counties Society* (HMSO, 1893–1902)

More, Sir John. *The Gentleman and Farmer's Friend* (London, 1712)

Philips, John. 'Cyder, A Poem' (London, 1708)

Salisbury, William. *Hints Addressed to Proprietors of Orchards* (London, 1816)

Trowbridge, J.M. *Cider Makers' Handbook* (New York, 1890)

Warcollier, J. *Ciderie* (Paris, 1928)

Worlidge, J. *Vinetum Britannicum or A Treatise of Cider* (London, 1678)

# Index

171

Mineral water manufacturers, 35, 84
Ministry of Food, 71, 72, 74
Morgan, Dorothy, 45
Morgan, Kathleen, 43
Motor lorries, 45, 69, 77, 78
Murphy & Son, 47
Murray & Co, Karachi, 39, 120

National Association of British Wine
  Producers, 141, 143
National Association of Cider Makers,
  44, 53, 67, 74, 76, 117, 136
National Association of English Cider
  Makers, 15
National Fruit & Cider Institute, 15, 78
Natural conditioning process, 9, 26
NAAFI, 86
Newfoundland, 14
Newton Abbot, 15, 20, 25, 63, 67
Newton, F., 56, 77, 91
Nine Elms goods depot, 35
Norfolk, 14, 15
Norman Conquest, 13
Norman, E. W., 118, 136
Nova Scotia, 9, 36, 39, 81

Oaff, Leslie, 53
Off-licence Protection Association, 50
Off-trade, 62
Oil engines, 64
On-trade, 62
Orange wine, 48
Orchard competitions, 47
Orchards, 21, 39, 47
Ordinary shares, 56
Ottery St Mary, Devon, 21

Paignton, 57, 66, 76, 79, 141
Parkinson, K. F., 137, 151
Peardrax, 89, 113, 114, 116, 127, 128,
  132, 147
Peaty, Malcolm J., 149
Pensions, 76
Pershore depot, 88, 92, 118
Petrol rationing, 70, 71, 75, 79, 88, 133
Philip Hill, Higginson & Erlangers, 110,
  113
Phipson & Co, 24, 39, 120
Phoenicians, 13
Phoenix Assurance Co, 76
Pig production, 72

Pipes, oak, 24
Plains, The, 15
Plumpton, Cullompton, 63
Plymouth, 22
Pomace, 30, 32
Pomona, 14, 87
Pomvita, apple liqueur, 38
Pony, British Sherry, 90, 114, 115, 116
Pope, C., 27
Poster campaign, 61, 62, 147
Potter, foreman, 27, 29, 30, 31
Poulter, John, 136, 137
Presses, apple, 20, 25, 58, 64
Price, Waterhouse & Co, 110, 113
Pring, N. W., 137, 151
Private company, 35
Public company, 55
Purchase Tax, 133

Quotas, customers', 71, 75

Railways: 15, 21, 33, 77; GWR, 56, 58;
  LMS, 52; L & SW, 20, 23, 27, 36, 38;
  Southern, 43
Raisin wine, 45, 141
Raleigh, Sir Walter, 14
Rationing, 69, 133
Reece, C., 77, 91, 118
Resale Price Maintenance, 116
Retail prices, 116
Rice, Miss Lilian, 67
Robins, Archie, 57, 67
Roche, George, 110, 111
Roman, 13, 20, 139
Rosewell, Peter, FCA, MBIM, 136, 137
Ross, Colin, BSc, 47
Rougemont Castle, 143, 145, 146, 147
Royal, Cyder, 14
Royal Wilding, 15
Rubery depot, 118
Ruby Wine, 60, 70, 81, 141

Sales, 20, 24, 27, 36, 42, 48, 62, 79, 86
Salesmen, 22, 44, 67, 71, 74, 79, 84,
  115, 116
Sales Conferences, 61, 70, 86, 114
Salvation Army, 37
Sanatogen Tonic Wine, 66, 70, 86, 113,
  127, 147
Savoy Hotel, 57, 58
Scandinavia, 14